Go Where They Are

By Dianne Morgan

www.womenterprises.com

Dedication

Dedicated with Love to God, Jesus,
and All who are seeking their truth.
My prayer is that all who are searching will discover
What you are searching for; and unveil the truth
That it has been within you all along.

Table of Contents

Dear Readers,

What is a Spiritual Awakening? It has been beautifully explained by many, for me I believe this is merely becoming aware and exploring your connection.

I am referring to Father-Mother God, Angels, the Archangels, Guides, Goddesses, Jesus and the Ascended Masters, all of the Spiritual Light Beings.

In 2015 I was called to teach others how to connect with the Spiritual Realm of the Angels and Archangels. The Spiritual Realm for me is a world that we can't physically see, that watches over us and guides us through life with unconditional love.

My belief is that the Awakening and the Spiritual Journey are as unique as you are. Seeking for your truth, what resonates within you, I explored and discovered there are many paths in finding your truth. I had begun my Spiritual Journey ten years prior, learning as I went, with the help of a dear friend and books; until I was guided to take workshops. Some call this guidance the Higher Power, some call it Spirit, for some this power, is known as Creator, or Source of All. For me this Higher Power I know as God. Using the term Spirit in these writings I am talking about connecting with all of the Light Beings, which for some is called heaven.

In seeking my truth, I had been led to consider many spiritual and religious beliefs from around the world. I had come to the conclusion that God is not a religion. There is more than one way to find your truth. One thing each religion had in common was the belief in a Higher Power guiding us.

5

In December of 2015 on a Sunday afternoon I was giving Angel Readings at a Holistic Festival when I was asked to speak about the Angels at the last minute. I felt uneasy as I had not prepared, I had no notes with me, no handouts. However; the desire in me to teach others was stronger than the hesitation, when I heard, "Go for it!" I walked into the classroom, and all eyes turned toward me, as I walked up to the front of the room, words that had never entered my thoughts came flowing out of my mouth.

"Good afternoon, I'm Dianne Morgan, and I am a Mystic Intuitive Spiritual Christian. I'm here to talk to you about God, and his Divine Messengers. Sorry to keep you waiting."

"Where did that statement come from?" I've gone back and forth with organized Religion since the age of fourteen. "Why would these words come out of my mouth?" "What exactly does the word Christian mean to me?" "How did I get here?" All these thoughts ran through my mind.

I discovered I had been on a life long journey with Spirit. It takes time to pull all those painful and hurtful memories to the surface to heal from them and transmute them into something positive. Yes, it is easier to bury them so deep you block them out of your world; however, they remain with you at a soul level and could be blocking you from finding the happiness you so desire and deserve until you choose to heal. Forgive yourself, forgive others and bring happiness to your life.

This is my story, the story of a seemingly average person (me) and everyday events through our lives that we write off as weird, strange, unusual, a close call, etc... Through countless conversations with the Archangel's I understand that we are all born with the ability to communicate with that Higher Power and the many helpers God sends us. Have you ever had something happen that couldn't be explained away by common sense?

Coincidence or freaky, just plain weird! However, somehow you knew it was a Higher Power at work.

The Spiritual Realm speaks to us every day of our lives. When we learn to pay attention we see, feel, know and hear the signs they give us. It's hard for some to believe this because they don't speak to us the way you expect them to, they don't pick up the cell phone and call us or text us. However, they do give us messages, and once I put all of this together, I was amazed to discover I had always been receiving information, just as you are. I just wasn't aware it was my connection with Spirit.

I am delighted to share my life long journey with Spirit with you. Reflecting on memories through my life when Spirit was working with me and for me, and I was unaware of it; then taking you through my awakening and some of the unusual events. My prayer is that by reading my story, you will reflect back and see how truly connected you to have always been.

May you enjoy reading how I learned that Father-Mother God, Great Spirit, Creator, and Source of ALL has always been connecting with each of us either directly or through messengers on this journey we call life.

Perhaps in some small way, it will help you know we all have a fascinating story to tell. Perhaps you will remember something that happened to you that you never associated a Higher Power guiding you. I pray that you awaken and work with your God-given ability and understand that you too can "Go Where They Are," to discover who you are for a fuller, happier, healthier life.

PART I
Reflections

Chapter 1
Years of the Past

In the first nine chapters, which we (Spirit & I) named Reflections; Spirit took me on a healing journey back in time; a journey through memories and events, which I saw in my mind's eye and some were long forgotten. I was also shown events which have helped me understand emotional issues that I wasn't aware of. Through my life I now understand Spirit was working with me all along.

Most understand that clairvoyance means premonitions of the future, but not always. I should explain that I now realize that I have been a Clairvoyant in respect to the dream world all of my life. I also understand that I am a claircognizance, which means; knowing things without knowing how I know them.

I am going to share memories with you, and some would argue perhaps they were imagined by an overactive mind. When I sat down at the computer it was as if someone was dictating to me; I began to call this, *"Angeltation."* As I was typing the words I heard I would recall the event I had long forgotten in great detail; the memory would play in my mind's eye like a movie, or a flash of the scene I had forgotten! I would ask Archangel Michael, "Does this go in the story?"

I would hear the reply, "Yes, you must trust. For the only way to understand who you are and move forward is to review and heal from the past."

To understand how I got to where I am on my journey, Spirit guided me back in time to relive events and emotions, back to the broken places so that I could understand God was always working for and with me and so that I could heal my heart and forgive. As I would start to remember the scene, I was watching the event, I was experiencing the emotions I felt at the time.

There was anger, hurt, tears, love and loss and many aha moments on this journey of rebirth. There were so many feelings and emotions of a broken soul buried so deep that I had forgotten the event and memory, until now, where I would finally feel forgiveness.

Funny, don't most of us do that? We only remember the good things in life, perhaps that is how we are wired so to speak, mask the pain to move forward, however; do we truly ever heal? Through this process, I was finally released, and forgiving myself and others for past hurts, while at the same time I was discovering I had been receiving guidance all through my life. Yes, like most of us, some of the advice I paid attention to, and some I ignored, and most I couldn't figure out how I knew what to do!

Spirit takes me to my first memory in my mind's eye, it was in December 1962, a few days before Christmas; I was the age of five. As the memory entered, I watched myself in bed sound asleep. It was well after midnight when I woke up to the sound of someone calling my name. Brenda, my older sister and I shared a bedroom, I sat up and rubbed my eyes then looked over at her, she was asleep. I listened, the house was silent.

Mom would tell you I was always hearing and talking to someone who wasn't physically there, which she could not explain who, how or why. As I lay there drifting back to sleep,

12

I heard my name again. I got up quietly and put on my robe then I softly opened the bedroom door. I crept down the hall and listened at my parent's door. I could hear my dad snoring. I tip-toed a little further to the door of the room my older brother Kevin and younger brother Bubba shared. I gingerly opened it, only to find them both sleeping. Bubba was always playing pranks on me. I whispered, "Bubba, was that you?"

He didn't answer; I stood there a minute then I gently shut the door. Just as I got it closed; I heard my name again, it sounded as if it was a breeze as it rushed past me and moved in front of me as if it were leading me. I followed the voice; my heart was racing. I stopped and listened again; it was coming from outside. I grew up in Houston, Texas at a time that it wasn't unusual for us to sleep with our doors unlocked. We never thought it was unsafe therefore; I had no fear of going outside in the middle of the night.

Hearing it now I can only describe it as a whisper traveling on the wind. I had to be quiet because if my dad caught out there in the middle of the night, well let's just say I was far more afraid of getting a spanking than going outside.

But the excitement inside of me was stronger than the fear of punishment. I tiptoed through the house to the front door. Someone outside was calling my name, and I had to see who it was. As I looked out the window, I saw the moon was full. I glanced around, but I didn't see anyone, yet again I heard my name in a sing song whisper. Perhaps most five-year-olds would have run back down the hall crawled into bed and put the covers over their head. Maybe they would have woken their parents. Not me, I was always the curious type, not afraid of anything.

13

I gently opened the front door then the screen door and slipped out onto the porch, careful not to let the screen shut on its own. I looked around and noticed there was frost on the ground.

The sky was in a brilliant glow as the moon glistened down on the frost. It was magical, a perfect Hallmark photo of a crisp winter night.

I have always been captivated by the moon it somehow speaks to me and draws me into its magical energy. I surveyed the yard and didn't see anything. Again, my attention went to the moon as I stepped off the porch and I stood there briefly admiring her perfect glow and how it lit the earth. Then I made out the image on the moon. Most of my friends said they saw a lady in the moon, but I always saw a picture of a long table with people sitting around, what I saw was the Lord's Last Supper. It seemed to bring peace inside, even at that young age.

My heart was pounding from the excitement racing through me to hurry; I knew I better get back inside before one of my parents woke and discovered me. I was shivering; my eyes were pooling from the cold air. My feet were freezing, when I looked down, I saw my bare feet. I had forgotten to put my slippers on.

All the urgency disappeared, and calmness entered as I gazed at the moon for another brief moment. Then I had the eerie feeling that someone was watching me; I looked across the yard when I saw a flash of light rush by me and then I saw a beautiful white wolf standing only a few feet from me. I blinked and wiped the tears from my eyes, and when I looked again, she was still there. My heart was pounding my eyes

14

watering. I wiped them again, I knew she was real and I wasn't afraid. I was elated. I always brought stray animals home, but, this was not a stray! She had called me out in the night to meet her, she knew my name, and I somehow knew she was here for me. She was magnificent! We stood only a few feet from each other, sharing a familiarity. I was thrilled!

I slowly approached, and in a small voice I said, "I won't hurt you."

Seeing her now in my mind, I had long forgotten how beautiful she was with her glowing robin egg blue eyes. From an early age, I knew I communicated with animals, but what was she trying to tell me? Then the wolf turned. My eyes followed her as she slowly moved toward the fence.

"No, please don't go," I pleaded.

She turned as if she was observing me, she lingered there for a moment again our eyes were in a connection of the soul. Then she began to move slowly again, and with one last glance over her shoulder at me, she looked as if she was smiling.

Then she jumped like a graceful gazelle into the air and over the fence. Was I to follow her? I watched as she mysteriously disappeared. No, she didn't run down the street, nothing like that. It was as if when she jumped she just vanished as quickly as she had arrived.

"Wait," I yelled as I ran across the yard and looked up into the sky. I woke my parents when I yelled. When I told my dad why I went outside, and what happened, he was not quite as excited as I was!

He said, "You must have been dreaming, there are no white wolves here. Go back to bed young lady." I heard him tell my mom, "She lives in a fairy tale. Now she thinks she sees white wolves."

To which my mom replied, "It was probably a dream, or it was one of her imaginary friend's. She's been talking to them all her life. You know she thinks they're real."

After a while I doubted myself, it's hard to believe in something when others have doubt. I wondered if my mom was right. Did I dream the incident? The vision drifted out of mind over time, and I had forgotten about it until 2013 when she appeared again!

That same winter now January 1963 we were on Winter Break, Kevin was building a boat. "Are you going to ride in it?" I asked.

He laughed at me, "Of course I am silly."

"I want to go."

"I don't know, we'll see. But not today the tar paper has to dry."

The next morning it was drizzly and cold, but I knew he was going to go out in his boat. I jumped up and ran down the hall. Both of my brothers were gone. We had a pond behind our house, and I knew where they were, they took the boat out to test it. They weren't going to leave me out! I pulled on my jeans and a sweatshirt, putting on my coat as I hurried through the house.

Brenda was making oatmeal, and as I ran by her she asked, "Where are you going?"

"Down to the pond," I answered as I ran out the backdoor.

I saw the two of them down on the bank when I got to the end of the trail; they already had the boat in the water. "Wait for me," I yelled as I began to run.

Kevin turned around and saw me, "Go home, it's freezing out here." He yelled.

"No, I want to go, if you don't take me, I'll tell mom and dad." He looked at Bubba, and with a big sigh, he replied, "Alright, you can go but one at a time, it's not big enough for three.

"Me first," I said as I pushed past Bubba.

Kevin climbed into the boat as he gave instructions to Bubba to hold the rope until he told him to throw it to him. "Climb in," he said to me, "but you better not tell mom we were out here." He made me pinky swear. Bubba held the boat as I climbed over the side. Bubba pushed us off and then through the rope; he watched as we started across the pond.

Looking at it now it was magical, the steam coming off the water made me feel like I was in a far away land. I pictured fairies leading the way in dance and a mermaid gliding across the water.

I pointed to her, "Look, see the mermaid!"

Kevin laughed, "There are no such things as mermaids Dianne, that's a floating tree branch with a piece of cloth wrapped around it." What he saw as an ordinary log, I saw as

17

a beautiful mermaid guiding us across the pond. As I looked across the water, it came to life in my mind.

We were in the middle of the pond when I realized my feet were wet. I looked down only to discover the homemade boat had a hole in it and was filling with water. Kevin noticed it about the same time. He began to paddle faster, turning us around to get back to the shore we started from, faster and faster, but not fast enough to overpower the water the little boat was taking on. We were almost to the shoreline when you guessed it! We were sinking! I stood up, and when I did, over we went into the cold water. The boat had flipped and was now on top of me. Panic filled me as I fought the water. It all happened so quickly. I was scared and began to cry. Then a soft voice from nowhere said, "I've got you. You're okay."

Maybe I blacked out I thought and it still feels like a dream, but seeing it now somehow the boat was lifted off of me and I was holding on. I heard Kevin calling me; I answered, and he swam around to where I was.

"Are you okay?" He screamed in panic.

"Yes," I quivered as I was trying to make logic out of what happened.

There we were in the cold pond holding on to an upside-down boat, using it like a barge. Kevin paddled with one hand and clung to me and the boat with the other until we were back on the shore. Now looking back, I heard someone speaking to me.

I wasn't sure why the next memory came to mind, many families break apart. It was now spring 1963, and my entire world was about to be turned upside down in my child's mind. I came home from playing at a friend's house, only to discover that my dad was leaving us.

He explained to Bubba and I that he had to go away for a while, that we were to mind our mother, and that Kevin would be the man of the house. Tears pooled in his eyes as he kissed my cheek and hugged me, then turned and hugged my mom who was holding back her tears. We watched as he walked away.

I was sobbing so hard, my heart as many little girls belonged to daddy, and I yelled, "Daddy, don't go." I tried to chase after him, but my mom held onto me as I cried.

Mom embraced me trying to sooth me; I kept asking, "Why?"

We all stood there and watched as daddy walked out of our lives. Mom took us into the house, and I went to my bedroom. When I entered, I noticed the room looked different. I walked back into the living room.

"Where's Brenda?" I asked my mom.

My mom opened her arms for me to come to her. We sat down on the couch as she wrapped me in her arms. We sat in that position for a few minutes. I looked up at my mom, and she too was crying as she wiped my tears and explained, "Brenda decided she wanted to live somewhere else honey."

"Why?" I asked.

"She wasn't happy here."

I sobbed so hard I was gasping for breath, "Why did they leave me? What did I do wrong?" I asked as I looked up at my mom.

"Oh, honey they didn't leave you, you didn't do anything wrong. Sometimes things just happen."

In the mind of a child, I thought *what did I do? Why did they both leave me?* I was lost, I went back to my bedroom now looking back it looked empty, and something in me broke that day.

As I am watching it now, I realized I was feeling, Abandonment! Wow, I didn't know I had abandonment issues. It was important for me to see this memory, to feel the pain again as it played a big part of whom I became in the future.

A major cut, a wound so deep that I stuffed it until I didn't recognize it was there.

My daddy walked away and the sister who I adored left me and never said goodbye, and never returned into my life.

As the days went by we were finding a new family dynamic, so many things changed in the blink of an eye. I was a child, and I didn't understand any of this.

Now I am seeing that next Christmas 1963 the Salvation Army brought me a Barbie Doll and a GI Joe in a Jeep for Bubba. We received boxes of food, canned meat and milk, and 5lb's packages of cheese, oranges, and apples.

I didn't understand any of it, but I remember I watched my mom cry in gratitude when they showed up. My mom

20

worked from morning to night, and still, she had a hard time making ends meet.

Was this memory to show me there is compassion?

In 1965 at the age of eighteen, Kevin quit school and got a job to help mom out. The war in Vietnam had begun, and because Kevin wasn't in school, he was called to go into the Army. The father replacement left, again I felt Abandoned.

It is now some forty plus years' later working on myself, healing of the heart that I finally understood what broke that day, it was trust.

I realize these are circumstances beyond my understanding at the time, but I now realize for many years this is why I began to check out so to speak from relationships for fear of getting hurt.

Self-preservation, leave them before they leave me. I have realized healing is part of the journey here and I have truly had to work on forgiveness of self and ask for forgiveness in all directions of time from those my actions have affected and yet I am still a work in progress. The spiritual journey is not only finding your path; it is uncovering what within yourself needs to be healed and forgiven, what needs to change within you so that you can move forward.

Now I'm being shown another dream. There was a car accident; I knew something was going to happen, I just knew. I couldn't see the people in my dream, but I saw an old car and a pickup truck. One vehicle ran a red light, and the oncoming vehicle crashed into the driver's side. I woke up; my heart was racing.

I had a creepy feeling, I got up and went and crawled in the bed with mom. She turned over and asked, "What's wrong?"

I told her about my dream. She listened and tried to help me understand, "You didn't see anyone in the car or truck?" She asked.

"No, but I saw the accident."

"Honey maybe it was something you saw on television."

"Maybe," I said questioningly as I snuggled up next to her.

"Let's try to go back to sleep," she said and gently kissed the top of my head.

It was three days later when I got off the school bus. I saw Mom's car was home, which was unusual. I ran into the house and found her sitting on the sofa rocking back and forth. She hugged me and sobbed as she told me my maternal grandfather had died in a car accident. Reports were he had just picked up his new glasses and was on his way home, he ran a red light and was hit broadside by a pickup truck in oncoming traffic. He died instantly.

When my mom told me, she looked at me in wonderment; it was just like in my dream. We lived twelve hours from my grandparents and saw them every couple of years, I had no idea what my grandfather drove. Later when I saw the newspaper clipping, I recognized it as the car from my dream.

I have since come to understand silence was my mom's way of protecting me from the judgment of others. She always listened and acknowledged what she called a gift most wouldn't understand. For fear of judgment I never felt safe in sharing my dreams with anyone other than my mom. After all, even Bubba thought it was weird when I would tell him I had known something before it happened. Thank you, Mom, for acknowledging this connection and listening to me; for believing me even though you didn't understand it. She said many times, "I don't know why or how." She believed me, her love, trust, and acceptance made it okay, Mom was always my safe place.

The next thing I saw was the Christmas after my dad moved back home in 1967. Bubba and I got a small piece of new found freedom. Bikes! Mine was a fire engine red, and Bubba's was a dark blue. We were so excited! We could hardly wait to ride them.

Dad said, "You can only go around the block, no further."

"Yes sir," we answered at the same time.

As we rode down the street, we grinned and waved at the neighbors. Oh, those were such carefree days. I remember the events of that ride; we went faster and faster. As we came to the curve, I took my hands off the handlebars and proclaimed "I forgot how much fun this is! Look I'm flying!"

Bubba laughed at me when I said, "No really we've done this before!"

"Whose bike?" he asked.

"I don't know," as I thought about it, I realized we had had this conversation before.

I dreamed it I thought. *"How do I know? How do I know we've done this before? Did I dream it before it happened?"* However, I knew we had been here before doing the same thing, having the same conversation.

"I guess I dreamed it," I answered. "I'm going back because in my dream there's a big brown dog down the road and he's going to chase us, and I got bit on the leg."

"You're so weird," Bubba said and laughed, as he peddled past me.

I stopped my bike and watched him go ahead. When he got to the end of the block, there he was; the big brown dog. He ran out onto the road and was chasing Bubba. I turned and went back the way we came. Bubba was in the driveway when I got there.

"Are you okay?"

"Yap, I'm fine. How'd you know about the dog? He looked at me in puzzlement. "Oh never mind. You're kooky." He said as he opened the gate he was mumbling to himself.

Once again, I had received the message in my dream world, which at the time had me stop and turn around so that I wouldn't get bit by the dog. Thank you, Spirit!

I was fourteen with the next vivid memory in 1971 comes in; at a pool party, everyone was taking their turn on the high dive. Even though I couldn't swim well, with a little peer pressure, I climbed the diving board ladder. Once at the top, even though I was afraid, I knew I had to jump. Everyone was watching me, and I couldn't back out now! I bounced a few times, and I jumped! I hit the water hard. Splat, landing right on my belly, of course, this knocked the breath out of me. I was going down gasping for air, down in a vortex, I was going to drown. In a panic, I was fighting the water.

I thought *I'm going to die* for what felt like several minutes. Then by some force, I was shooting to the top, I looked around thinking someone had pulled me up. But the lifeguard was swimming toward me, and there was no physical being around me!

The lifeguard asked, "Are you Okay?"

Shaken and embarrassed I shook my head "yes." He helped me to the side of the pool and out of the water; my best friend Tiffany ran over to me and handed me a towel. We sat there for a few minutes as I wiped my face.

"Wow, are you okay? What happened?" She asked.

I answered, "I hit the water on my stomach, and it knocked the breath out of me."

"Ouch! You sure you're okay?"

I shook my head and answered, "I'm fine. Who jumped in and pulled me up?"

"The lifeguard," she answered.

"No, before the lifeguard, someone pulled me up?" I said.

She gave me a look of concern, "No one," she answered, "Maybe you hit your head?" I answered her, "I'm just a little shaky." as I sat there I wondered *who or what lifted me up above the water?*

It was Spring Break 1975, I was now eighteen. One afternoon a group of us were on our way home from the beach. My boyfriend Ray and I were involved in a car accident with an eighteen-wheeler. The truck was headed right toward us, and I saw something shinny like metal or were they lights? Next it felt like we were lifted up and pushed out of the path.

Then we swerved, and I flew up and then down onto the floorboard as we went bouncing across a cow pasture. Yes, pasture, in Texas it is not uncommon for the FM's (farm to market roads) to be lined with fields. When we stopped, I was sitting on the floor, with a large knot on my head the size of a goose egg. Ray's white knuckles held onto the steering wheel in a death grip.

Once the police came and questioned us, we were all allowed to leave; Ray was still in a state of disbelief as he nervously rambled, "I thought we were going to die, scared the crap out of me. It was insane; I didn't know I swerved, it felt like a gust of wind carried my pickup truck and then we were bouncing across the field."

I smiled as I held the icepack to my forehead, and answered, "I know, I felt it too." We had both experienced something, but neither of us was sure what

CHAPTER 2
Free Will in Motion

The next event has played in my mind often throughout my life, so it was no surprise that I was guided to share it with you.

It was around my twentieth birthday. I was in a cold sweat when I woke up in the middle of the night from a dream. In the dream, I was at a funeral home, and there were two women in the room standing by a casket. I couldn't see the body in the coffin. Who had died? The two women in the dream stood with their backs to me, *who were they?*

I couldn't see their faces. One woman spoke to the other, and I knew the voice but who was it? I heard her voice cracking when she said, "We should have an anchor of red, white and blue carnations made, for his service in the Navy."

When I woke engulfed with a chill, my Uncle Bob popped into my mind. He had been in the Navy, but also he had a lot of medical problems.

I didn't know what to do. It reminded me of the dream long ago of my grandfather's accident, no details as to whom; but a heads-up that something was going to happen. It took me a while to go back to sleep, as I drifted off I questioned who was in my dream.

The next morning, I woke up and the dream was replaying in my mind.

I asked myself. "What can I do, am I supposed to tell my family I had the dream?

Now a newlywed, my husband Andrew who was a 5'9 handsome dark featured man had overheard me talking to myself, he stuck his head in the bathroom door and asked, "Are you talking to me?"

"No," I replied, "I was just trying to figure out a strange dream I had last night."

"Sometimes a dream is just a dream," he replied as he walked into the bathroom and kissed the top of my head.

I hadn't told him I had been having dreams since my childhood and that many times what I dreamed played out in reality. I had learned through the years not to tell people the things I knew for fear that they would think I was weird. I wonder what he would have thought if I had? I thought about it for a minute and then came to the conclusion that I didn't know when or if this was going to happen or who was in the casket; so it would be best if I said nothing to anyone.

It was about two weeks later, January 16, 1977; it was a cold, wet Sunday morning. I had woke up suddenly around 7:30 AM with a dreadful feeling that something was terribly wrong, but as I laid there I shook it off so to speak and decided I should try to go back to sleep. The phone rang around 8:30 AM, and I was thankful it was on Andrew's side of the bed, and I didn't have to get up to answer it.

In my slumber, I couldn't make out everything, but I overheard heard Andrew ask, "When?"

Then I heard him say, "Okay, we'll be on our way. No, she's still sleeping. Okay,"

He paused then whispered, "Okay, I will."

I rolled over and asked, "What is it?"

"Your Dad," he answered.

With a sigh, I said, "It's too early. What does daddy want now?" I pulled the pillow over my head, and I rolled back over to continue this wonderful lazy Sunday morning sleep.

He wrapped his arms around, and held me for a brief moment when he whispered, "No, that was your mom babe," and he paused then he said, "It's your Dad; he's had a heart attack."

I jumped up, "What? What hospital? We need to hurry." I said as I ran to the closet and grabbed a pair of jeans. As I was pulling on my jeans and looking for a t-shirt in a panic, Andrew walked up behind me, touched my shoulder.

"Babe," he gently said.

I knew what he was trying to tell me, but I wouldn't look at him because if I did, then it would be confirmed in his eyes.

"Hurry up and get dressed," I said.

"Babe," he paused still touching my shoulder, "He didn't make it."

"What?" I questioned puzzlingly, "He didn't make what?"

I turned, and he was standing in front of me, "I mean, he didn't survive the heart attack, he died around 7:30 this morning."

I began to shake my head, "No, no, you're wrong, we need to go," as I grabbed my jacket and hurried out the door.

29

There was no conversation during the drive to my parent's home. I kept thinking *it can't be true; he's not dead, they're wrong.* I wasn't crying; I was numb, I didn't believe it.

The sheriff car and the ambulance were in the drive when we pulled up. I jumped out of the car and ran past the paramedics, into the house. I entered the front of my childhood home, there was no-one there. I could hear voices at the back of the house. I ran down the hall someone grabbed me as I went toward the bedroom.

"This is my family, where is my daddy?" I lurched, "Let me go."

Mom looked up and noticed that someone had stopped me and I was fighting my way into the room.

I heard her whisper, "Let her in."

The deputy released my arm, where I saw Mom and Bubba sitting on the side of the bed leaning against each other. When they looked up at me, the expression in their red tear stained eyes confirmed what deep inside I already knew. Daddy was gone.

I walked through the bedroom into the bathroom, there was my dad lying motionless on the floor.

With a shaken voice, I yelled, "Daddy," getting louder with each cry, "Daddy," until I was screaming at him, "Daddy, get up!"

Then I started to crumble to my knees, Andrew had somehow made his way in and luckily caught me before I hit the floor. I must have gone into shock because everything forward on that day escapes me with exception to the next dream.

That night we spent the night with my mom and my dad came to me in my dream world, he was laughing and telling me he was fine as he started to leave, I cried, "Don't go daddy." I woke and sat up as I looked around the room I noticed specks of light, which I would later discover are called orbs. With tears in my eyes, "Daddy," I lightly whispered. I know what I saw was real, and sweet as he said goodbye to me and exited this physical plan. Seeing it now is once again a confirmation of how real it was.

Once the autopsy was completed and reported dad died from a massive heart attack, his body was released. Mom, my Aunt Lue (dad's sister) and I went to make final arrangements at the funeral home located at the cemetery. As I stood there looking down at my father's corpse, my heart was shattered into a million pieces. Even though ours was a conflicted relationship through the years, he was my dad and I loved him. As a child he was my first hero, and I couldn't even imagine not hearing his laugh or one of his corny jokes again. With tears running down my cheeks I turned and sat down on the front pew.

Mom and Aunt Lue stood at the casket talking. I was lost in my heartache when I heard my Aunt Lue say, "We should have an anchor made of red, white, and blue carnations for his service in the Navy."

I froze, then I looked up, their backs were to me; I couldn't catch my breath. I got up and ran out of the funeral home. I couldn't stop; I ran across the cemetery grounds and ended up down by the little lake where I knew my dad would be. I looked around, but he wasn't there. I had to sit down, I found a bench, and that is where I was sobbing uncontrollably when my mom found me.

She sat down beside me and took my hand, then wrapped her arms around me and she said, "Honey, breath."

We sat there together as my heart bled, not only of lose but of guilt; the wall I had built around my heart in the last few days now tumbled down into a river of tears.

Mom comforted me, "I wondered if you were going to keep holding it in or let it out. You haven't cried. Let it out baby girl." There we sat in the middle of these beautiful grounds, my mom holding me in her arms as I wept.

As she held me, I said, "I should have known it was him. Why didn't I know?"

She asked, "Honey, what are you talking about?"

Through my sobs, I explained, "Mom, I had a dream, I couldn't see who was in the casket in my dream. But when I heard Aunt Lue talking about the anchor it all came back to me and played in my mind in slow motion. It was daddy, why didn't I know it was daddy?"

My mom held me and soothed me, "Shoo, honey," she pulled a tissue out and wiped my tears and then continued, "Even if you knew it was your daddy, you couldn't have prevented it from happening. He wouldn't have listened to you; he wouldn't have gone to a doctor, we both know that."

We sat there for some time in silence.

I saw my Aunt Lue walking toward us, mom smiled and softly asked me, "Are we ready to go now?" We got up and walked arm and arm to the car.

I knew she was right, but still, I did not understand why I had these dreams or why I saw certain things but not actual people. After the event at the Funeral Home, I made the statement to my mom, "I don't want to see things in my dreams before they happen if I can't change them!"

Through my spiritual journey and studying the act of Free Will it dawned on me that was the day I shut my clairvoyance down. I now understand the Law of Attraction, and when I spoke those words I put my Free Will into motion, and God and the Universe said, "Okay."

I shut down from communicating with Spirit through my dream world. That doesn't mean I wasn't still connected as we all are. I asked not to see information if I couldn't change the outcome and with that, the dreams did stop, until much later in my life.

33

Another incident with my dad happened a few weeks after the funeral. I was standing at the front of the building I worked at, gazing out the window when I saw my dad's truck. He was behind the wheel and smiled that million-dollar smile. Without a thought, I ran outside the building and yelled at him to stop then I helplessly watched as he waved goodbye and drove away.

Also, Uncle Bob died within that year, and he too had an anchor of red, white and blue carnations.

CHAPTER 3
Motherhood

We moved in with mom one month after the funeral; I suppose we all needed to be with each other. Andrew and I discussed having a baby, we weren't trying, but if it happened, it happened.

Within a month my body began to feel different, I hadn't missed a period, but I knew I was pregnant; I made an appointment. When I explained to the doctor I was pregnant, he ran the test, and said he'd be back with the results. He came back a half an hour later, "Well, I'm afraid you're mistaken, the test is negative."

I shrugged and declared, "Doesn't matter what the test reports, I don't know how I know, but I'm pregnant."

To that, he smiled, and began to explain the hormones, then added, "Make another appointment in about two weeks, and we'll run the test again."

Danielle, with this beautiful dark hair, and hazel eyes was born in December of that year, on dad's birthday! Her birth brought so much joy and helped make the holidays a little brighter for all of us. I believe that was Spirit at work. I knew I was pregnant about a month before the test proved positive.

Mom and I both wrapped ourselves up in this beautiful new little bundle of pure joy, with her big green, yet blue eyes that seemed to shine. When Danielle was six months old, I went back to work, and Mom decided to retire, she stayed home and watched after this sweet little new life which she had become very attached to.

One evening we were all watching television in the front of the house. It was after 10:00 pm when we heard Danielle laughing down the hall. There were no baby monitors at the time and I went to check on her. When I entered the room it was cold and I swear I saw colored lights on the ceiling. I looked over at the baby lamp on the dresser but it wasn't on. That was weird, but another thing even stranger was the rocking chair. It was moving slowly back and forth and immediately stopped when I walked in the room. That put a fright in me; I grabbed my daughter and walked briskly to the front of the house.

Andrew laughed at me and then went to double check the room and came back to tell us the bulb in the lamp was just loose and was flickering when he entered the room. He said, "You must have just thought you saw that chair moving in the shadows of the flickering light." That was entirely logical, and I agreed that he was probably right even though I had the strangest feeling there was something more to it.

Over the years I now understand, it was my dad. He now rocks in the rocker on my front porch every day watching the lake and naturally he would have come to visit his grandchild.

Again, time kept marching on, and within two years from moving in, Andrew and I saved enough money to buy our first home. On the day of the move, I was following behind in my car. Andrew was driving the moving truck. Danielle who was standing up next to me in the front seat, long before mandatory laws of children in car seats or riding in the front seats, we didn't even know what airbags were. I was singing with the radio, and making funny faces to make Danielle giggle. We were several cars behind Andrew and the moving truck when a vehicle came from nowhere and darted in front of me to make the next exit. I hit the brakes at seventy-five mph, which caused Danielle to go flying forward. I reached for her and saw what I described as a flash of light, as it was happening I thought we were crashing into the other vehicle. I grabbed her with one hand and steered with the other when what looked like a white light moved in front of her as if something blocked her from going through the windshield and diverted her into the floor board. Needless to say, I was shaking and in disbelief as I pulled to a stop on the shoulder of the highway. I began to check Danielle who was lying in the floorboard crying. I thought *just like the accident where I ended up in the floor board.* Danielle did graze her head on the dashboard as she fell to the floor. She had a little bump on her forehead, and that was it!

Andrew never saw what happened and by the time we got to the house, her little bump was now the size of a small egg. Still pretty shook up I tried to explain what had happened.

Andrew took Danielle as he grinned and said, "it all happened so fast you just thought you saw a white light. The first instinct is to close your eyes when you know there is going to be a crash.

I thought *maybe he's right!*

Not long after this we were on that same highway and the front tire came off and went flying past us, and we managed to get to the side of the road safely, and no other vehicles were involved.

These events could have gone much worse without the help of our guardian's that come with us at birth. Our loving Creator sends us into this world with protection. Angels or Guardian Angels were protecting us, and no one or nothing will change my feelings on that!

My second pregnancy was in 1979. I have not shared this part of my life with many people, until now. However, writing it I now realize it is a significant detail in my healing process, and again some will find this unbelievable, and some will identify with the event in many ways.

This pregnancy felt different from the start. One morning during my sixth month, while getting ready for my regular doctor's appointment I had the strangest knowing something was wrong. When the doctor examined me, he asked, "Have you had any twinges or pain?"

I replied, "No, I feel something is different, but no pain." He proceeded to tell me that I was in labor, and I would need to be admitted to the hospital immediately. I began to cry, as I thought *I'm only in my sixth month.*

I now realize how truly naïve I was; I had very few life lessons or experiences. Although I claimed no organized religion and had a personal relationship with God, my doctor and my husband were Catholic, so here I was in labor at a Catholic hospital that had religious beliefs against ending the pregnancy. As my doctor explained, the pregnancy was terminating itself, and he was more worried about me than the baby at this point. At this moment, the memory of the conversation brings tears to my eyes; my heart was breaking into zillions of pieces as I heard that my child wouldn't survive and there was absolutely nothing that could be done to save the baby.

I had been in labor six tormenting hours, going through the pain of labor was nothing compared to the ache I harbored in the cavern of my heart. I wanted to scream, to shout, to throw a fit, to make someone do something that would change the outcome. My mind was ranting; *Why didn't I know? I didn't take any extra precautions. I lifted my two-year-old, I carried groceries, cleaned house, and I moved file boxes at work.* The thoughts kept coming in *did I cause this to happen?* Soon I was blaming myself. My heart was breaking as I laid there in my self-guilt. The priest for the hospital came by, and we talked and prayed. He explained that they would baptize the baby and handle all the arrangements. I know by this point I was in a state of shock, asking why, why, why?

When it was time to deliver the baby, I was taken to the operating room and hooked up to numerous machines. The last thing I remember was praying for this little soul. I knew this baby wasn't going to live, that I was never going to hold this child in my arms or watch it grow up or just be its Mom. I asked God to take care of this unborn child when I began drifting into a drug induced state that cast this little soul and me into a spinning dark tunnel, when I saw something ahead. *What was that?* I thought as I saw the light; I was floating, gliding, I heard the most beautiful music. Up ahead I could see a brighter light, a golden light at the end of the tunnel. There was a strong desire to go into that light, the overwhelming feeling from within that I had to reach it. I kept floating like a feather floats on a breeze, moving slowly toward that golden light. As I got closer the light became brighter and brighter, yet so beautiful; it was a pure golden blinding yet tranquil light.

I paused at the end of the tunnel when I saw a golden glowing hand that reached out to me through the light. There was a feeling of unconditional inexplicable love that washed over me; somehow this warmth of love embraced me. However; somehow, I knew that even though I wanted to, I couldn't accept this hand. With hesitation, I spoke softly, "I can't go yet. I have a daughter, and I can't leave her."

I stood there crying and torn while basking in the light, what should I do? Go or stay? Within I knew the choice was mine. It also felt that on some level I was saying goodbye. By not reaching out and embracing the hand, I had made or affirmed my decision to stay.

Suddenly it felt as if a vacuum sucked me backward. The next thing I knew I was hovering over my body, yet something wasn't right. I heard someone say, "Pressure is dropping, we're losing her."

Then with a jolt, I was back in my body and aware of everything going on around me. I was conscious, and yet bewildered. As I laid there I wondered *what had just happened! Was it Real or Did I dream it?*

Later that evening I tried to explain what I experienced with my doctor.

"Did something happen to me in the delivery room?" I asked.

He said, "Nothing to be alarmed about."

"But something strange happened, I think I died, I saw a tunnel of light, and then I was floating over my body."

He smiled, patted my hand and said, "You were under anesthetic. Some people have that feeling."

I didn't accept his explanation something was urging me to explore it deeper. Over the years I discussed it with a few family and friends, some who found it odd but had no explanation. Others called it my near-death experience.

I, however, know what I experienced that day and what I saw truly occurred.

We never saw our child; we did discover it was a little boy, he weighed under a pound, his fingers and toes were still webbed. Perhaps the doctor was right when he suggested it would not be a good idea to see the baby. I was already blaming myself, and that picture would haunt both of us for the rest of our days. They never asked for a name, and hence baptized him as Baby Boy; he had a name, his name in my heart is Brandon, not Baby Boy. The hospital took care of all the arrangements and his death was listed as "not a vital fetus."

The doctor tried to explain what had happened. After this pregnancy, I was diagnosed with an incompetent cervix, in short, this means that the cervix was open, allowing air in and affecting the baby's brain. He said that if the baby would have survived he would have suffered brain damage. His belief was that this was why my body aborted the baby. It was no one's fault. But yet I felt it was my fault, somehow, someway I caused this to happen.

41

A few days later it was such an empty yet heavy feeling on the drive home from the hospital in a silence that engulfed me. A silence that I took was a confirmation that Andrew also blamed me for the loss.

I blamed myself; therefore, I was confident that he blamed me, and it was far easier not to discuss it then to put all those emotions on the table. I carried my guilt. Eventually, over time I buried it. I convinced myself that God knew I would have suffered more had something been wrong with my child, rather than never know my child at all. I felt it was his way of protecting me.

I, however, discovered many years later that I did not forgive myself. I pushed this profound heartbreak so deep until the time came to heal.

Again, another loss in my life that was suppressed, not even mentioned.

Spirit works in the most unusual ways; there was a post shared on social media tonight, the very night I put my feelings into words. I would like to share part of it with you.

 Remember all babies born sleeping, or those we've carried but never met, those we've held but couldn't take home, and the ones that came home but didn't stay. The post was asking that we share the message because unlike cancer, the discussion of miscarriage, stillbirth, and SIDS are all still a taboo subject.

Break the silence, in memory of all angels too perfect for the earth. I pray that in some small way someone or many, reading this will began to heal their hearts. Knowing that you are not alone, talk to your spouse, find a support group and express your feelings so that you may begin to heal.

In 1982 I was expecting our third child, due to the incompetent cervix this time I had numerous problems during the first trimester of pregnancy. I had to have a procedure called the Macdonald Stitch, to help me carry the baby and I was put on complete bed rest during my third month of pregnancy. I have to tell you I was scared to death; the question "will I carry this baby full term," worried me every day. I tried not to buy into the fear of losing another child.

I had Faith in a Higher Power and Positive thinking. I prayed daily for a healthy baby. I followed the doctor's orders and got up to go to the restroom or grab something out of the refrigerator to eat. I did not cook, clean, or do laundry. Danielle was now five. A few days a week one of her Grandma's would pick her up, but on the days, she was there, she became my mother and tried to take care of me.

She would sit on the floor by my bed and play with her dolls, color or watch TV while I slept. She would take everything out and put it on the counter and then wake me when she was hungry with everything ready for lunch to be made. We lived on cereal, peanut butter and jelly sandwiches and noodle soup, her favorite foods at the time.

In the afternoon, she'd crawl up on the bed with me for her nap, and then she'd sit there on the floor playing until her daddy came home from work. I must have slept eighteen hours a day, but you know, we do what we have to do, and we made it work, and for the next four months, this was our life.

Finally, I made it to my third trimester, and I could get up a little more as we were out of the woods so to speak. The ultrasound was new, and it predicted we had a son coming. However, I somehow didn't think this was a boy. I hoped Andrew wasn't disappointed. I also had a feeling I wasn't going to carry the baby full term.

It was about six weeks later when a burst of energy came over me; I woke up early and began what some call "nesting." The next day at thirty-four and a half weeks I went for a routine doctor's appointment when he once again asked me had I had any pain.

"No, I feel good." I answered, and then asked, "Why?"

"Honey, you're in labor, this baby is going to be a little early, but you're far enough along that we have no major concerns."

I continued to pray asking God for everything to be okay and believed that it would be. We had our third child, a beautiful blonde, blue eyed, 3lb 11 oz. Baby Girl, we named her Anne. She had to stay in the hospital until she weighed 5lb's, but otherwise, she was healthy. I went home again for the second time without a baby, but this time knowing I had a healthy baby that just needed a little more time to grow. I went to the hospital twice a day, every day, to feed her, rock her, and sing to her. Bonding, in the beginning, is so crucial for the mother and the child's relationship.

Six weeks later my prayers were answered, and my intuition was correct, we took our beautiful, healthy baby girl home!

This was truly God at work.

The next event that runs through my memory occurs in early January 1985. A typically hectic day in our household, we had a new addition, our youngest child, Adam, was about six weeks old, my beautiful little boy, he had Andrews olive skin and darker features with exception to the eyes, he had my deep ocean blue peepers. On this particular day, my fifth-teen year old sister-in-law, Marcie, had come to visit and needless to say, I was thrilled to have the help for a few days.

That afternoon I laid down for a nap with my two-year-old, after a few hours I woke up with the oddest feeling. It was after 5:00 pm. I was in a fog, something felt wrong. When I walked out of the bedroom, Adam was bundled and sleeping on the couch. I asked Marcie, "When was the last time he ate?"

She said she had tried to feed him an hour ago, but he had only taken about an ounce and went back to sleep.

I sat down on the couch and picked him up; something didn't feel right in the pit of my stomach. With the experience of losing one child and having now had two premature babies, I was a little more than overprotective.

I tried to wake him and tried to feed him, I lifted his little arm, and it was as if it had a weight attached as it fell back down. I tried numerous times; he would open his little eyes briefly and then fall back asleep. Something was wrong, within minutes I put a call into the pediatrician. I tried to call Andrew, but he had already left work.

I paced back and forth at the same time trying to wake him as I waited for the pediatrician to call back, that fifteen minutes felt like days. When she called, I explained to her what was going on with him, and she advised he was probably fine.

"I'm sure it's nothing serious, keep an eye on him, but he'll probably wake up screaming and starving anytime," she said.

The next hour and a half came around, and he still had not awakened; now I was afraid that there was something terribly wrong, my intuition was yelling at me "this is not normal!"

We had one car, and it was now almost 7:00 pm. I tried to stay calm, I had started dinner and Marcie kept the girls occupied.

When Andrew walked in, I was still pacing back and forth holding Adam and trying not to panic. He immediately saw the concern in my eyes as he hugged our girls.

"What's wrong?" Andrew asked.

"He's not waking up to eat, and he can't keep his eyes open."

"What'd the doctor say?"

I explained the previous phone call, "Well, then he's probably okay, just tired," Andrew said.

"I'm calling her again, I know she said he was probably fine, but that was a few hours ago, and I can't shake this. I know something is wrong with him. He still hasn't woken up, and now he's lethargic."

Andrew was calm, "Dianne, the doctor said he was probably fine. You were at my grandma's all day yesterday. He's probably just tired or maybe he's catching a cold. If he doesn't improve take him to the doctor in the morning."

46

But I couldn't shake what I knew and I handed him to Andrew then went to the kitchen to the phone. This time when I called the answering service picked up, they told me she was on duty at the hospital. I explained I had talked to her earlier and it was important that I speak with her now. I asked them to page her. She must have been standing by a phone because the phone rang within five minutes. "Hello, this is Dr. Stevens."

"Yes Doctor Stevens this is Dianne again, Adam still hasn't woken up, and now he's lethargic. I think something is wrong." I sniffled through my tears.

With a concerned tone, she advised that we get him to the emergency room. Of course, now I was terrified, we all were. Marcie would stay with the girls, feed them and get them ready for bed.

Andrew and I bundled up and got into the car; this was long before there were hospitals conveniently located around town. We had a forty-five-mile drive.

Several things happened on the way to the hospital on this cold winter night; my son stopped breathing in my arms. I started to cry as I talked to him and jiggled him around then he'd gasped a little whimper. I had to keep moving him to keep him breathing, my heart sinking with each breath.

Next, our car began to overheat. Andrew said, "I don't think we were going to make it."

With tears streaming down my cheeks, I closed my eyes and whispered, "Dear God, Please help us."

When I opened my eyes, and looked up, I saw the exit to the street where mom lived. I said, "Get off here, we'll borrow Mom's car."

He immediately exited the highway and as soon as we pulled off the feeder road and onto the street, the car stopped. Mom lived at the other end of the block. Yes, I could have stayed in the car out of the cold wind, but there was no time to think. I was doing what I was being guided to do.

It was near forty degrees outside, and the temperature was dropping, not to mention windy, damp and dark.

In a panic, I wrapped Adam up against me and buttoned my coat with him inside. We got out and started walking as fast as we could against the cold wind as it gusted around us. I continued to bounce him as I walked I had to keep him breathing. When the thought came to ask someone to let us use a phone, "It's so cold out here." I said through shivering teeth.

Andrew said, "I told you to wait in the car."

Then I saw a light, and I pointed to a house. "Maybe we should ask if we can use the phone and call mom and she can pick us up." We knocked and pleaded at the first house. Someone peeked out but wouldn't come to the door, the same thing happened at the second house we went to. No-one would open their doors.

I realized it was dark and we were stranger's, but couldn't they see we needed help! Finally, we came to the house of Mrs. Maxine Tinsley. She had lived there since I was a child. I was apprehensive to go to her door. She was the grouchy old lady back then, a widow that lived at the end of the street.

She was never too friendly. She dressed like an old witch and scared us at Halloween and squirted us with the water hose when we got to close to her house. The lady we were all afraid of when we were kids. I said, "Andrew wait, not this house, she won't let us in."

He ignored me and walked up on the porch and began to bang on the door. Mrs. Tinsley peeked out from behind the drapes. By now he was yelling, "We need to use the phone, we have a sick baby."

She cracked the door, and asked, "Who are you?"

"Ms. Maxine, its Dianne, remember I use to live down the road. Our son is sick we're trying to get him to the hospital, but our car broke down. Can we use your phone to call mama? Please?"

She opened the door a little wider and took a good look at me. Once she realized who I was, she said, "You Fern's daughter?"

"Yes, ma'am," I answered.

She opened the door and scooped us in out of the cold. When I told her what was wrong, she handed Andrew the phone. I was crying and praying as I held and bounced my son, looking at this tiny life and so afraid he was going to stop breathing again, and so very grateful to have him inside out of the cold. All my childhood fear of her vanished as I gazed upon her with kindness.

I don't know, but now I look back at this moment as a lesson of not judging others. Mom was there within a few minutes, and we were on our way again. By the time we got to the hospital, it was almost 10:00 pm. Mom and I got out at the emergency room door, while Andrew parked the car. As I began to explain to the nurse, another nurse rushed up and grabbed Adam and went straight to the back with him. I heard them paging Dr. Stevens as Andrew walked in the automatic door.

Mom sat with me while he went to call his mom. I couldn't sit still. I felt completely helpless. I looked around a few minutes later. What was going on? What was wrong with my baby? I couldn't sit. I got up and paced back and forth asking, "God, please let him be okay."

We were all trying to stay calm, and then I looked up and saw a Priest coming down the hall toward us. That's when I lost it. I watched as he stopped short and turned and went into the room where they had taken Adam. A Catholic hospital and seeing the Priest my first thought was last rites or baptism, he didn't make it. I hit the floor on my knees and began to scream hysterically, "God, Nooooo, Please Don't Take Him; Pleeeeease, Not Again!"

A nurse ran over to where I sat on the floor. Andrew was crying as he and the nurse helped me up and over to a chair. I felt lost as I sat there and sobbed as I rocked myself. Andrew whispered, "I'll be back." I couldn't tell you how long he was gone or when he returned; he later explained he had gone to the Chapel to pray.

My mother-in-law got there shortly after and in that waiting room, the minutes felt like hours and hours seemed like an eternity. Finally, shortly after 11:00 pm Dr. Stevens came out to talk to us.

"He has bronchial pneumonia," she explained, "the x-ray shows he has milk in his lungs. He stopped breathing on us a few times back there. As per the hospital's policy, we called the Priest. But you have a little fighter! We've started him on a very strong antibiotic. He's under oxygen. The next twenty-four hours will be critical."

I was confused; I had never heard of anything like this. I asked, "How could milk get in the lungs?"

She explained, "This happens with some premature babies, they forget to hold their breathing when they are suckling, and when that happens they inhale milk instead of air."

She patted my hand, "As I said he's a fighter. We're moving him up to Infant Intensive Care Unit on the sixth floor. Let us get him settled in up there and then you can see him."

Andrew said, "Thank you, Doctor." I smiled and shook my head in agreement. Dr. Steve's touched my arm, "I'll see you up there in a few minutes."

We rode the elevator up to the sixth floor and waited in the waiting room. We were no strangers to the Infant ICU, with Anne and Adam's premature births we had been here. I just didn't realize we would be back here so soon.

A half an hour later we were standing over the little bed, and I had my hand inside the arm hole as I held Adam's little fingers, and stroked his hand. He was so very tiny as I looked upon him and he struggled to breath. I closed my eyes and whispered, "Thank You."

We settled in for the night; I was not leaving my baby.

Our prayers had been heard and answered. Adam stayed in the hospital for three weeks. I believe if I had not trusted the guidance that night we might have lost him, of course at the time I didn't realize Spirit was communicating with me.

Again, I followed my intuition and again trusted in what I somehow knew, and felt. He wasn't meant to transcend that night and Spirit, and I worked together to see that, that didn't happen.

There are so many things that happen in our life every day that we don't think about; things that we are being guided from another realm, being lead to the right answers. Thank You, God!

CHAPTER 4
Beginning a New Chapter

As the years went by Andrew and I grew apart, in different directions if you will. It was no one's fault, we each wanted different things, had different goals for the future. I felt that I had lost Dianne somewhere along the way. I honestly did not know who I was anymore. I was someone's wife, daughter, and mother, but who was Dianne? I wasn't happy, and couldn't imagine spending the rest of my life unhappy. It was my decision to divorce.

Two and a half years later in 1987 at the age of thirty, I now found myself a single parent of three. The kids would visit Andrew every other weekend as per the court agreement.

In the beginning, after the divorce, I spent more time with mom. She kept insisting that the kids and I move in with her. I kept insisting that was not an option. I thanked her, but I was determined I could do it alone.

Shortly after the divorce, I had worked my way up the ladder so to speak and was now a Branch Manager in a male dominated industry. One thing my dad taught me is to do the job well, and I could do anything I set my mind too regardless of my gender. I now had a good salary, more than I had ever made, but that wasn't enough for a family of four. I took a few part time jobs here and there. I had always believed that children should not have to lower their standards of living due to divorce.

Mom worried about me, not only because I was her daughter but because she too had been a single parent and knew how stressful and hard it could be. She expressed her concerns often, and I always responded with "I believe that God will take care of it, somehow, some way."

In one conversation, she asked me, "Where did your Faith come from?"

I smiled, and replied, "Mom, I'd like to think in part that it came from you, Grandma, Granny Whitaker and from life. My faith tells me, and I just know, I don't know how to explain it, I just know God is a loving God, and he will watch over me. I trust in that."

He always has, even in the darkest hours he was with me, the good and the bad he has never left me. The answers to problems were just there in my head, and I just knew what to do. The money I needed always seemed to arrive. Not that I didn't work my tail off putting in sixteen-hour days, sometime working two jobs; and thank goodness I was able to find good honest women to live-in and take care of my family.

I will admit this was one of the hardest times in my life and as I think back now I could have done some things differently, like spent more time with my children, more time at home. However, I do believe that we do what we feel is best at the time and learn the lessons. After all, at that age I felt I had all the time in the world, and then one day we look up, and our children are adults. I had found a freedom that I had never known. I moved from my childhood home at nineteen and went from my dad telling me what to do and taking care of me to a husband. I had always had someone to take care of me. Now by my own choice, it was all on me.

Over time my lifestyle began to change. I eventually started going out with friends and dating. At first, I drank socially which eventually led to drinking alone, which resulted in depression.

Being the bread winner, the mom, the dad, doing it all, this was hard. I worried and stressed out over having enough money to pay the bills, and there were times I wanted to give up. I convinced myself that I drank to cope, to take the edge off, and to relax. As the months came and went again two years had passed, now 1989 Andrew had remarried. I admit there were times I thought perhaps the kids would be better off with him in his traditional household. I questioned myself on this topic daily, but even though I didn't spend much time with them, when it came down to it I loved them. They were my babies, and I couldn't imagine them not in my day to day life. I wanted to share life with them every day, even if some day's it was only a kiss goodnight.

At the time, I was searching for myself, searching for what was going to make me happy. Seeing the change in me mom made the comment, "You were a different person when you were married to Andrew. Now we have Dianne back, and I don't know that the world is ready for that!" We both laughed.

Little did she know I didn't know who that was, I guess she did. Not knowing what I was searching for led me in many directions until I found home within myself many years down the road.

CHAPTER 5
Judgment Comes So Easy!

I am guided to share this for you to understand the importance it played for me putting the puzzle of myself together to arrive where I am today. There are times that events are nothing more than lessons we came here to learn.

Yes, life as we knew it had changed, however, I realize I wasn't paying attention and didn't notice the changes that were going on with Bubba. We never talked about our feelings about dad's death. Which was the norm for my family, we didn't talk about feelings at all.

After daddy had died; Bubba had dulled his pain differently, he had gotten involved with drugs. Andrew and I had been called over there a few times due to his outburst and disturbing behavior. Bubba never moved away from home, maybe he thought mom needed him, but I felt they were both afraid to go forward with life. A co-dependent relationship, Bubba needed someone to take care of him, and mom needed to be a caregiver. I didn't know the extent of his drug abuse, and I assumed he was just smoking pot, taking speed now and then and drinking, that's what he told me and I believed him. I might not agree with it but who was I to judge him.

After a while, he started selling pot, which I was soon to find out led to his involvement in something far deeper than mom or I had known.

March 1992 mom called me at work, and asked me to come over she said: "He's talking crazy, and I'm a little scared of him."

I heard it in her voice; she was frightened. "Bubba's always listened to you. You're the only one that can talk to him. ."

I left work early and drove the hour's distance in Houston traffic. When I got there I looked in his room, he was lying in bed wide eyed staring at the television. He looked up and hatefully said, "What are you doing here."

I recall the wild look in his eyes, these eyes' I did not know. My heart shattered as these were hollow eyes of a stranger. This was a shadow of my brother who was in some drug induced state, which alarmed me that he was involved with more than pot. But unlike my mom I wasn't afraid, I was mad! Me being me, I replied, "What do you think you're doing?"

He said, "None of your business. Get out of here."

I answered, "You are my business, and you scared Mom, and she called me. That's why I'm here."

He was yelling at me, "What's she afraid of, I'm not hurting anyone! You need to mind my own business and go away. You don't live here. You left! So what do you care?"

I yelled back at him, "Okay, you're right I don't live here, and if you want to destroy your life well fine. But think of what you're doing to mom."

This time he was hateful as he swung off the bed and yelled, "I'm not doing anything to her. Just leave me alone!"

There was a fiery look in his eyes, but I couldn't back down from him. I didn't know if he was going to lash out and hit me but at this point, I didn't care.

I was yelling at him, "I'll get out when you get up and start acting like a man and stop hiding behind drugs! Are you that angry, that depressed, if you are then you need help!"

He jumped up; he looked at me with a hatred I had never experienced from him. He pushed his way past me but not before he said, "You don't know what you're talking about, you don't know me. I'm not your problem. You always think you can save everyone. Well not this time sis, not this time." He walked outside to the garage and slammed the door behind him. Minutes later I heard his Harley fire up.

I was shocked and furious as I returned to the living room. "Mom you should kick him out. Maybe that would get his attention!"

Her reply was, "I know, but at least when he's here I know he's alive and not in a ditch dead somewhere. I know it's just his way of dealing with things, I've been hoping and praying that he would get it out of his system, but it's getting worse."

"Mom, it's been years since daddy died. At first, I could agree he was numbing the pain, but not now, he's not going to change. He needs help."

"I know." She answered.

I left shortly after that with nothing resolved. *When did this happen* was my thought on the drive home. *Had I been so absorbed with my own life that I checked out of his? Why is it my responsibility? Because somehow, some way I had always felt Bubba was my responsibility.*

Five Months Later

Everything on the surface appeared to be okay and perhaps improving with Bubba, there had been no more incidents. Then the phone rang at 4:45 AM one morning.

I was in the bathroom getting ready for work I glanced at the clock *who's not coming in today?* I thought. It wasn't unusual for my employees to call me at home if they were going to be late, or not going to make it in that day.

"Hello," I answered.

"Dianne." I knew the moment I heard mom's voice something was wrong.

"What is it, Mom? What's wrong?"

She hesitated and then answered, "They arrested Bubba yesterday, and I just got home from the Police Station."

"What happened?" I asked.

She said, "I guess you didn't see the news."

I had gone out that evening, so I had missed the news.

"No, I wasn't home," I answered.

Then she began to tell me the story. "It was just after lunch when the dogs started barking, and I heard a gunshot. When I looked out, I saw the police in the yard, and they shot Fishy, in the leg. I yelled for Bubba when the bullets started flying. I crawled down on the floor as bullets rang through the air." Her voice broke at this point, and I could tell she was crying, "I was scared to death. I didn't know what was going on when they came through the front door with guns pointed at me and ready to shoot."

As she was telling me I could see my 68-year-old mother on the floor, my heart was pounding, and I was so angry with Bubba.

"Mom what happened, why'd they shoot the dog, and raid your house?" I demanded.

"They arrested Bubba," she began to cry.

"Was he selling marijuana?" I asked.

"No, it is far worse."

"What, mom, what'd he do?"

"He had Cocaine and Marijuana, but they had a warrant for his arrest for two counts of armed robbery and impersonating a DEA Agent."

Needless to say, I was in shock, this couldn't be happening. I knew he was into drugs but this was beyond my thinking, this was major! "Mom, why were you at the police station? Did they arrest you?"

"No, Bubba told them, I didn't know anything about it. But they took me into the police station for questioning; it was all so unreal. Hours of the same questions until they finally let me go. Then I spent hours waiting for them to set Bubba's bail. I have to go back after the bank opens and I can get the cash. I just knew something was going to happen, that he would end up in jail. I've already talked to his friend Bill and hired an attorney."

She sighed, "It was all on the news. The officer they interviewed said they had been watching the house for months and reported that it was a resident of a drug ring dealer. They showed Bubba handcuffed and as they put him in the police car he looked over his shoulder directly into the camera. His eyes were full of hatred; I didn't recognize my own son."

Bubba got out on a bond later that night and was going to trial in sixty days. The state offered him a plea bargain. The detectives flat out told him they didn't want him; they wanted his boss. They wanted him to help catch him, or they would see to it he went to prison for a very long time. They wanted Bubba to work with them to take down the head of the drug ring. That was when I realized he had gotten involved in something that he felt trapped him, something far bigger than he was.

Over the next weeks, Bubba naturally went through a rough patch of detox. We all knew he was going to prison. He would get a lesser sentence if he agreed to set up and catch the person's the authorities were after. I tried talking to him about it, and through one of these conversations, I discovered the armed robbery charge was for stealing drugs from a Dealer at gunpoint while posing as a DEA Agent for another Dealer. This was not the life I knew, and it all sounded like a movie, I couldn't even picture my younger brother doing these things.

However, I also now understood his comment months ago. "You don't know me or what you're talking about. I'm not your problem. You always think you can save everyone. Well not this time sis, not this time." As the words hit me again, this is when I realized I didn't know this man at all and no I couldn't save him.

I asked him why he wouldn't work with the detectives and give them the information they wanted, if it meant he would get a better deal? I didn't get it, and I wanted to understand what had happened to him.

"The people they want are ruthless people, if I rat them out, I won't last a day, and you, your children and mom would be looking over your shoulder for the rest of your lives. If anything happened to any of you, I couldn't live with myself. I'll take my chances; I'm not a snitch. I am guilty, and I will do time. I'll be okay."

 For all he was and all he had done, he loved his family. Even though I saw what I describe as a hatred that had brewed in his heart, for that one brief moment, he allowed me to see a glimpse of the brother I knew. Regardless of the things he had done he wasn't thinking of himself. He was truthful and thinking of his family. But why did he have such a wall around him that as hard as I tried to understand him, I couldn't penetrate that wall.

What caused him to walk this path? I could still see this darkness about him, he cared for us his family, but he didn't care anything about himself or humanity. I was still angry with him for involving mom. I loved him or who he was, and I was thankful that I got to spend time with him before he went to prison. I didn't know when, or if I would see him again.

I didn't attend the trial which lasted three short days. Bubba pled guilty, and the State showed that he held someone at gunpoint, that he was wearing a DEA jacket and stole the drugs. When in fact we all knew, he was supplied drugs to commit felonies' but he contended he did it all on his own free will. In October 1992, he was sentenced to two twenty year back to back prison sentences. He would be an old man when he got out if he ever got out.

When mom called to tell me the outcome I felt the feeling of guilt as it washed over me. I hadn't been there for my Mom or Bubba. Could I have made a difference? My gut was telling me something was going on with Bubba, but all I could see were the drugs. Why didn't I know? I have since learned that toxins prevent us from hearing Spirit. My day started with two cups of coffee (toxin) a couple of cigarettes (toxin). I skipped lunch most of the time, and I had a minimum three glasses of wine at night to chill out.

What made me any different from him? We had both found a way to dull the pain and deal with life.

Who was I to judge him?

Events, Lessons and Memories: Angels Were Truly Watching Over Me

It was around a month later on a Saturday afternoon, and the kids were with Andrew for the weekend. I went out with a group of girlfriends. Innocent enough, first it was Christmas shopping, then dinner and then we decided to go for a few drinks. Before the afternoon was over, we visited every bar on the street. None of us were ready to call it a day, and someone had the bright idea, "let's go dancing!" And dance we did, until the wee hours of the morning.

63

I woke up buck naked in my bed around 2:00 pm the next afternoon. I looked around and wondered *how did I get home?* Oh, I was hung-over, holding my head, I got up and went to get a drink of water and then opened the medicine cabinet to find two aspirin. When I closed the door I stopped, I saw a stranger looking back at me, "Who are you?" I asked as I gazed at myself.

I walked downstairs and saw my clothes strung across the floor and the door to my patio home was standing wide open. I began to remember driving home, *what time was it when I got home* I wondered as I shut the door and said, "Thank you, God." Once again I knew a Higher Power was watching over me. I remembered leaving the club, the valet brought the car and we all jumped into the back seat. It took my friends a few minutes to convince me it was my car and I had to drive.

"I can't keep doing this. I have three babies that depend on me. What was I thinking...or was I thinking?" Of course, I was thinking, and everything in me knew this was my road to walk, and I had to get it together.

But not yet, there were still lessons to learn to lead me to where I am today. What next?

Another event the end of that year that comes marching through my mind is when Mark (a tall, hazel eyed, good looking man I had been dating off and on for a couple of years) and I were on our way to spend the weekend on his boat. We saw an accident on the Interstate. "Get off at the next exit, I know another way." I suggested.

Mark looked over at me, "It's getting dark maybe we should just ride it out."

64

Rather than sit in the bumper to bumper traffic, I convinced him to get off the highway and take the back roads.

As we were driving on the Farm to Market Road, he commented, "This is in the middle of nowhere, no wonder there's no traffic on it. There's nothing out here."

I laughed, "Trust me."

It was getting dark. As we rounded a curve, there was a car heading straight toward us.

I braced myself I knew this was going to be bad. I screamed, "Oh God Nooooo!"

I immediately saw a flash of bright light and instinctively I covered my eyes. I felt the impact of the truck as it turned and slid, the other vehicle clipped us and then we slid to a stop.

I saw a flash which I assumed was fire. When I opened my eyes, I expected to see flames. But instead, Mark's truck was turned sideways in the middle of the road. The other vehicle was in the ditch with smoke coming out of the radiator.

Mark asked, "Are you okay?"

I looked around and nodded yes.

"I don't believe it! We slide around, and he clipped the front fender which sent him flying into the ditch, and us to a stop."

I had just been in another head-on auto accident similar to the one I walked away from unharmed when I was a teenager. I had just seen something stop the collision. One might think I would have stopped at this point and realized someone was watching over me. In the accidents, I had been drinking and not paying attention. However, I now believe Archangel Michael stood between the vehicles in those accidents because it wasn't my time. Just think if I had been sober the amazing story I would have to tell you about seeing Archangel Michael stop those cars!

After I had begun teaching I had a student that told a story of an accident she and her daughter were in, she asked, "Does Archangel Michael, stand with a giant piece of shiny metal to protect us? Because I swear, I saw what looked to be like an Angel with a shiny piece of metal stop that other car from hitting us."

I laughed and answered, "Well, actually Archangel Michael carries a Shield of Divine Light which to the human eye could look like shiny metal. I have also seen it. My thought is Yes it was Archangel Michael." I have heard that the only time Archangel's intervene in our lives is in a life or death situation that would terminate our life prematurely.

I recall the next event New Years Eve past midnight; it is now 1993. Mark and I were celebrating at the lake, after the celebration at the adjacent hotel we started popping fireworks. We walked out to the end of the peninsula to pop them over water. Across the cove, maybe fifty feet away was a Marina. I had the bright idea to hold the bottle and shoot the bottle rocket, which was okay until I pointed one and it was traveling directly toward the gas pumps located on the dock, at the Marina!

Mark yelled, "Ooooh No! Run!"

I stood there in disbelief, he grabbed my hand, but I was stuck in one spot, mesmerized by the bottle rocket's path. Mark turned to look at me then back across to the pump, and at the very last second, we watched as a gust of wind turned the bottle rocket to the right of the pump and directed it into the water.

We both stood there our mouths agape.

"WOW," he said, "I don't believe it! You're a nut! I thought you were going to blow up the gas pump and us as well! Do you have like special powers, or a guardian angel or something?"

I laughed, winked and answered, "Or something."

Then we both chuckled.

We spent most weekends on Marks' boat over the next two years until he sold it due to financial difficulties in the late spring of 1995. But not before once again another event occurred. This time I was half asleep and I walked off the back of the boat in the wee hours of the morning, of course, the water woke me up fast!

I panicked for a moment, and then I heard, "You can drown, and no one will ever know what happened to you, or you can swim to the back of the boat and get out." I am not a strong swimmer, and always said: "I can't swim."

But that moment I told myself, "I can swim!" So, swim I did. I reached the back of the boat and pulled myself out of the water. I was okay.

I received the encouragement from Spirit and the power of positive affirmation! Was it Archangel Michael's protection once again, or was it my Guardian Angel encouraging me that I could do this. Regardless, something was driving me to take action. Angels are around us all every minute of the day, and sometimes I was paying attention and took action on the messages and other times I didn't. I had yet to realize this was Divine Guidance.

There were always incidents of unexplainable outcomes. Again, thank you to the Angels for watching over us.

Mark's business was declining. We had been going together now for several years, and it seemed like the logical choice to invite him to move in with the kids and me. I wasn't aware until after the fact that my girls felt I should have talked it over with them. Shortly after he moved in the kids announced they wanted to go live with Andrew.

In a conversation, I told Mark, "I guess I am from an entirely different planet because the thought never crossed my mind to ask my children how they would feel about it. Perhaps that was because my parents never asked my permission, or discussed their decisions about anything with us. We were the children, and they were the adults, end of story."

I now realize I was in denial at the time, and it wasn't just Mark moving in; it was me, my whole lifestyle. I hired a Nanny to do all the things for them I should have been doing. I made certain they had a beautiful place to live, food and clothing. When they weren't with Andrew, I took them to my mom's. So, in honesty, I spent very little time with them over the last eight years. I was not taking my responsibility as their mother and feeling their emotional nurturing needs.

Looking back through the years I know I could have and should have handled it differently. However, this event was a wake-up call.

At first, I thought maybe it was a good idea for them to live with Andrew. It would give me a break; I would have more me time, I wouldn't have to be responsible 24/7. Andrew and I discussed a joint custody arrangement, six months with him six months with me. I called my attorney, and after a brief conversation, he advised me that if I left them with Andrew for six months without going back to court, he could file abandonment charges against me and I would lose custody of my children. I couldn't afford to go back to court, and when I mentioned it to Andrew, he didn't have the money to go back to court, but he also kept insisting that the kids asked him if they could come live with him.

What happened next was truly God's work. I was sitting out on my patio I heard a voice, "If you do not like the direction your life is taking perhaps it is time to review or examine your decisions and choices to discover what needs changing."

Over the next few weeks, I took a tough look at my life. I had to make some changes. I loved my children, and I wanted the chance to be the mother they deserved. I prayed to God to give me that chance. To be the mother, I knew I could be. After this the answer was clear. I decided the answer was, No, I wouldn't lose my children, and I didn't think it was fair to ask them to choose between the two of us. So in my heart, I did the best thing as their mother and decided for them.

I believe at that time God knew I needed a life review. He knows my heart, and when I asked for help it was painful, I had so much guilt for not putting my children first. Now years later after studying the angels I know, it was one of God's messengers. It was Archangel Jeremiel's voice I heard, offering me a life review so that I could see how my choices had created this situation. Through this review, it was easy for me to see I was not happy and these three lives meant more to me than the lifestyle I had chosen. I was still searching for myself, but one thing I knew, was that what I was doing wasn't working. It was time for change.

CHAPTER 6
Everything Changes

May of 1995, I was in the process of purchasing my first home. I had been ready to move from the area we were in, but because Danielle was in high school, I chose to stay so that she could graduate with her friends. Since the divorce we had moved around often the first few years, we had been in this house for five years, and I was ready to buy something. The new home was a promise I had made to the kids, along with letting the Nanny go. We would stay in the same school district, and Anne and Adam would be continuing school with friends they had known since elementary.

Now, mind you this was a quick timeframe. I didn't know if Mark would move with us, but I knew that I had to keep moving forward with and for my children.

A week after graduation we moved into our beautiful four-bedroom home, me, the kids and Mark.

Mom had lived in the same house since 1960 and was now the age of seventy-two, with numerous health issues I worried about her being by herself; however, I knew the decision was hers to make. I planted the seed, and a few months later she moved in with us.

The first two and a half years passed and all was well. Mom and I became friends during these years, expressing our deep feelings about life in general, and our beliefs. Decades later she told me how angry she was with my dad for leaving her.

She said, "My first thought was, what now? My future that I saw had changed in seconds. He lied to me; he promised to grow old with me. I was so damn mad at him for dying."

My thoughts were, *he didn't leave you. How could you be angry with him for dying? Death is a natural process of life.*

I didn't understand her anger. I tried to think this through, long before I studied the five stages of grief. I now realize anger is natural, and long before I experienced my first emotion of anger that someone died.

I had lost also, and it had broken me in ways I hadn't yet understood. Not to be able to give my dad a kiss on the cheek, have him hug me, or play with my children. I somehow have always known that death wasn't the end; that we would reunite with loved ones.

I have never visited his grave. I know with my being that nothing is there but a marker. Our bodies turn to dust, and our souls are with our Creator. I don't have a need to visit a stone slab.

1999

The days rolled into months and years. As time passed, it seemed that mom was becoming more forgetful not only with the present but also memories that she had a hard time recalling. Not only her mind but her body was also rebelling against her with rheumatoid athirst, lupus, and diabetes. Her knees were breaking down, and she was in constant pain, and the medications just weren't helping her.

One day after she had been to her doctor she announced, "I've decided to have knee replacement surgery. I have to have some relief, and Dr. Roark has scheduled the surgery for two weeks from tomorrow."

Her knee surgery went smoothly, and mom was expected to have a full recovery. There would be weeks of physical therapy, besides some pain and discomfort for a few weeks.

At home, I had arranged for a neighbor to come in and fix meals. She arrived at 9:00 and left at 3:00 when the teenagers came home, and I would be home around 6:00 pm.

The physical therapist came every other day. Things weren't going as they had anticipated. Mom was making a slow recovery.

Eight weeks had passed, and she was still on the pain medication and using a walker. She could get up and fix her meals and insisted she didn't need a nursemaid.

One morning something was urging me to call home, and when I did, there was no answer. I tried several times then knew I needed to go check on her. When I arrived, I found my mother lying on the floor crying. I ran to her, "Mom what happened?"

Mom looked very confused when she answered, "I don't know. I stood up and fell and couldn't get back up."

As I was helping her up I asked, "Why didn't you use the walker?"

She looked at me like I was speaking a foreign language and then asked, "What Walker?"

She had forgotten that she couldn't walk by herself.

Now I once again say "Thank You God." for giving me the message to go home that morning. She could have lay there for hours, or worse, she might have tried to get up and walk again and fell and busted her head or hip. Any number of things could have happened.

Mom slowly recovered from the surgery, which did not end all of her pain, however; her memory continued to worry me, there were many more episodes, which the kids lovingly called, "Grandma's Spells."

She would be okay for a while then out of nowhere she would ramble on subjects and events that we didn't know anything about, and she continually forgot simple things. Through time someone had to be with her 24/7. The neighbor friend would again come in and visit with her daily until the kids came home. Then I would take over from the time I got home until I left for work. I knew I couldn't keep up this schedule; I was so emotionally tired and would start crying over the least little thing. I thought if I could just get a good night sleep I'll be okay. Mark suggested that I go to the doctor and find out what was going on with me.

I eventually made myself a doctor's appointment, and when I told him why I was there, we had a lengthy conversation, he diagnosed me with anxiety, and he advised me my blood pressure was stroke level, he prescribed two blood pressure medications, and an anti-anxiety medication. I was to make a follow-up appointment in two weeks.

I had to get some rest; I asked Danielle to come home for the weekend and help with mom. Friday night I slept ten hours, and by Saturday morning I felt better. Late Saturday night

Danielle knocked on the bedroom door, waking Mark and me.

She gently opened the door and whispered, "Mom."

I heard Mark ask her, "What's wrong?"

"Grandma wants Mom," she was giggling, "she's talking crazy, and keeps yelling for Mom. She said I had to find Dianne. She keeps saying they are going to arrest her, and she told me to go get Dianne before the Military Police got there."

"I'm coming," I answered as I got up. It took me some time before I finally got mom to settle down and at 3:30 AM, the house was calm once again.

These episodes lasted several months, every day a new day. Some day's she appeared to be fine, and others well not so much.

After one of her spells, I found her sitting on the side of the bed staring out the window. I sat down beside her, held her hand and asked, "Mom, what's wrong?"

"I'm losing my mind," she said tearfully, "I know it, and there's nothing I can do to stop it."

As I sat and held her, we cried together.

Mark and I had been together through all of this. He would help where he could, but most of all he helped me emotionally. I found what an incredible, compassionate, loving man he is and in March 2000 we married. Mom was my matron of honor, and she was having a good day. It wasn't long after this Mark received a job offer from an oil company. The position was for a construction project for a refinery in Syria. We discussed it and agreed that it was an opportunity for us to put some money aside for our future. He left the end of September and would be on a month on month off rotation schedule.

Mom would have a few good days, but when the bad day came, it was chaos. Our new norm as the year 2000 came to a close, and we were now in 2001.

Mark had been home from Syria for his rotation when all lives changed on 911. He would not be returning. Due to the security of the situation in the Middle East the oil company pulled all their employees out. He had now been home for over a month, we had discussed moving and made the decision to relocate to Canyon Lake, Texas located between San Antonio and Austin. Mark's childhood dream was to live in Canyon Lake, and I thought maybe it would be good for all of us. We would move with Adam and mom; we had found a house and had planned to remodel and make a two bedroom into a three-bedroom home to have room for everyone.

October 2001

For you to understand the messages I received, I am guided to share this part of my life with you.

I had decided to leave work early, just a feeling that I needed to go home. I had learned if I had a gut feeling I had to listen to it. When I entered the house, all was quiet, Anne was watching TV, and Adam was at basketball practice. I looked in and found mom taking an afternoon nap. I changed clothes and went downstairs to start dinner. An hour or so passed when I went to look in on mom I found her lying there staring at the ceiling.

When she noticed me; she began to speak in a disoriented fashion; she slurred her speech and wasn't making any sense.

I ran to the phone and dialed 911 "I believe my mom's had a stroke."

At the hospital, the doctor explained that mom had a mini stroke, and apparently not the first one, he wanted to run a regiment of test to confirm the diagnosis and check a few things. She would be there several days.

When I explained it to mom, she just nodded her head in confusion and answered, "Okay."

Two days later my secretary buzzed into my office, "There's a Dr. Roark on line two, he says it's about your mom."

I was a little nervous; my gut was telling me this was going to be bad news. I was not ready for this conversation.

I picked up the phone and nervously answered, "Hello this is Dianne."

"Ms. Morgan this is Dr. Roark; I have the results from the test we ran on your mother. She suffered a mini stroke, better known as a TIA. We also found something else" he paused. "There's no easy way to say this, so I will just say it. All tests show that your mother has dementia.

Dr. Roark continued, "Ms. Morgan, are you still there?"

I couldn't think, I was speechless, "Yes, yes doctor." I stuttered.

As he spoke, my mind was drifting. I wasn't listening as my thoughts were going back to all the events that led up to this conversation.

I'm still not sure what he said, lost in my thoughts and then I heard his voice again as he was saying something about "the mini stroke combined with dementia" When I tuned back in I heard him say, "She'll have moments when she knows you and other times when she won't. Eventually, the moments of not knowing will override the knowing. Sadly, that is how the disease progresses. Symptoms include problems with memory, judgment, and thinking. As the stages progress, memory loss becomes more apparent, in time she won't recognize any of her family or her surroundings. I am sorry to say there is no cure for dementia."

I vaguely remember saying, "I understand."

"Ms. Morgan, there are numerous support groups I can recommend. I know you have a million questions, so why don't we set up an appointment and discuss the options."

"I'll do that doctor, thank you." and I hung up.

I sat at my desk as the tears began to spill and ran like a wave down my face. I was speechless. *How am I going to explain this, what am I going to say?* Her words 'I'm losing my mind,' played back to me, when something strange happened. I saw a room of windows with a closed metal door. I didn't have a clue why this flashed in my mind.

I stopped at the hospital to visit mom that evening. Dr. Roark was coming out of her room, seeing the distress in my eyes, he smiled and asked, "Can I speak to you a moment?" I nodded my head as I followed him down the hall to a visitor's lounge. We sat down, and he gently said, "Ms. Morgan you can't continue to take care of her by yourself. It takes five adults around the clock to do what you are trying to do alone, and I can see it's affecting your health. If you're sick who will take care of you? How long has it been since you had a check up much less a good night's sleep?"

It's true I thought, and then the flood gate opened. I began to cry and unload all my emotions on to the doctor.

"Mom only wants me to do for her and no one else. She yells for me at all hours of the night. She forgets the simplest everyday things. I've started dead bolting the doors in fear that she'll forget where she is and wonder off. She forgets she has to use a walker and has fallen numerous times. I found her lying on the floor in the living room one morning. I'm afraid to sleep."

As the words left my mouth and it was at that moment, I realized once again I had to make some changes. I had to find a safe place for mom.

He explained that he could sign the orders to send her to rehab from the hospital. She would be there for two weeks, which would give me some time to figure out what I needed to do.

With Bubba being in prison there was no way to discuss this with him. I contacted Kevin and Brenda. After telling them what the doctor was recommending they both agreed that I had no choice, as neither was in a position to help with her.

By this time, we had already put a contract in on the house in Canyon Lake. There was no way I was going to leave mom in Houston; I didn't want to be that far away from her. She was

79

moved to a temporary rehab center the following afternoon. At the center, I spoke with the Social Worker, and she began searching for facilities in New Braunfels, Texas which would be close to where we were moving. There were only two, one had no beds available, and the other would have a bed in a week. I drove to New Braunfels and visited the facility.

The Manor was clean; the staff was friendly. I paid attention to the residents and didn't notice any neglect. I felt we found a good place for mom to live and proceeded with the red tape involved. Now to tell her, this was going to hurt all our hearts. I would wait until the next weekend when I would tell her and drive her to New Braunfels.

On Saturday morning I walked into mom's room, "Hello."

"Hi, did you come to take me home?"

I sat down on the side of her bed to explain the new situation. I couldn't find the words. When I did, she was quiet. I explained, "Since we were moving I found a place in New Braunfels where you will be close to me."

"When do I have to go?" She uttered.

"We're leaving as soon as I can check you out of here."

Mom only said two words, "I understand," as a tear fell and flowed down her cheek.

It was a long quiet drive to her new residence in New Braunfels. Both of us lost in our thoughts. *Was she upset? Was she afraid?* I was taking her hundreds of miles away, and promising we would be there soon. I wondered if she was thinking of her mother. My grandmother was in her late 80's when she began to have mini strokes and then developed Alzheimer's. My mom and her siblings had to make the same decision.

I prayed she understood what I was doing was in her best interest, and how it hurt me so deeply to do this. I was guilty that I could no longer take care of her, guilty that I was taking her away from everything and everyone that she knew.

We closed on our new home in December 2001. After the move, I continued working with the same company with the exception that now I traveled visiting branches in Texas, Oklahoma and New Mexico teaching operation procedures. However, it allowed me the freedom of working from home when I needed to be there.

For a while, I think mom was happy, she had made some new friends and joined the Red Hat Club. All was going okay until the end of 2002 when the mini strokes returned and the dementia seemed to get worse.

In March of 2003 Mark had gone back overseas this time the job was in Iraq rebuilding the war zone. I can't say that I was not concerned. However, I knew this was something he wanted to do, and I supported his decision. This position would be three months there and fourteen days home. Once again I found myself in the lead role of the household.

One afternoon I was on my way to our corporate office, a three-and-a-half-hour drive from New Braunfels when I received a phone call from the nursing home. Mom was at the emergency room. She became very agitated and combative.

I turned around and headed for the hospital. When I arrived, I could hear my mom yelling from one of the rooms. I walked in and immediately saw the terror in her eyes.

Trying to help I walked over and brushed her hair to soothe her. I thought, seeing me would calm her. She looked up at me and began to yell ugly profanities. I had never heard her curse like that, nor had she ever cursed at me. She slapped me on the cheek and screamed at me to get out. Stunned I backed out of the room in tears, feeling defeated I slid down the wall to the floor. Someone came over to me and put her hand on my arm. "Honey, she doesn't know what she's saying."

I thought; *"I have never seen my mom like this."* Then I said, "She's never talked to me like that." I wiped my eyes, "Logically I know she doesn't know what she's saying, but she didn't know who I was."

They had given her a sedative and had taken her for a battery of routine test. I was in the waiting room when a nurse finally came to give me an update.

"Your mom is in a room, you can see her, but she's pretty drowsy. The doctor will be up there shortly to talk with you."

I cracked the door and peeked in the room; she smiled at me, the smile of kindness you give a stranger in passing.

I said, "Hi, how do you feel?"

"Tired," she answered then asked, "Are you, my nurse?"

My eyes begin to swell up, but I smiled and said, "Yes, can I get you anything?"

She shook her head "no," I smiled and patted her hand, "get some rest. Call me if you need anything."

I turned and walked out with tears rolling down my cheeks. I sniffled as I stood outside her door. I thought, *this is the first time she hasn't recognized me. I know that that woman in there is not the mom that raised me. She's lost inside her mind.*

Suddenly I understood the vision I had seen some time back. Which I now understand was Spirit showing me what happens to those with dementia. My understanding of dementia was like being locked in a room full of windows. One could see out yet was trapped inside because the metal door to the outside world was too heavy to open. Occasionally you could push it just enough to crack it open, then it would slam shut again.

I cleared my thoughts as the doctor walked up and he began to explain. "Mrs. Morgan, your mom has suffered a mini stroke."

"Yes, she's been having them for some time, but I have never seen her like that."

"Due to the severity of this mini stroke, we're going to keep her a few days for monitoring."

I heard him, but for a split second my mind flashed to the room with all the windows and the metal door again.

The Power of Faith

In late 2003 mom was admitted once again to the hospital only this time it was for pneumonia. I arrived and walked around the bed, she was asleep, and as I stood there looking down at her, she looked so frail. She was on oxygen and hooked up to various monitors. The nurses must have told the doctor I was there; he came in and asked if he could have a word with me in the hall. I followed him out the door when he turned and said, "She's in pretty bad shape. I've got her on antibiotics and oxygen to help her breath easier. You might want to notify family to come."

I looked at him in dismay as these words spilled out, "I will call them, but Doctor, My Lord is not taking her today. He knows I am not ready!"

Yes, I was still holding on to my faith and hope. I fully expected mom to wake up and be herself again. I supposed this is what I had been waiting for the last four years.

The look on his face was priceless, not knowing how to respond to my affirmation. When he finally did speak, it was soft, he repeated, "Your mother is very ill, I don't think she will make it through the night. I am sorry." He touched my shoulder then turned and walked away.

Of course, I called my family to tell them that mom was in the hospital with pneumonia she was very weak, and the doctor said the outcome didn't look good. I called the prison and asked the Chaplin to give the message to Bubba. It was now around 9:00 pm as I sat there and watched mom sleeping, she looked so weak, so tiny. I began to pray.

"Dear God, I know you answer prayers, and I am asking for one of your miracles. Please, send your healing. Please heal her Lord. I know it's in your time, but Father I am not ready to lose her, and I just know the doctor is wrong."

Mine wasn't the only pray that night. There were prayers in the masses, with family and friends praying for her all over the country.

Various family members did come to see her that night; she would smile and then drift back off to sleep. We took turns napping and continued talking to mom even though she faded in and out all night. The next afternoon mom opened her eyes. She looked around confused and then asked, "Can I have something to drink?"

I laughed and kissed her forehead, then held the cup to her lips as she sipped the water. I buzzed the nurse's station and asked that they let the doctor know she was awake, talking and thirsty. I was feeding her Jell-O when the doctor walked in, he looked at mom and then at me and smiled as he proclaimed, "I need the list."

In puzzlement, I asked, "What list?"

"The prayer list," he said. "I honestly didn't feel she would make it through the night. I want the list of names because if I ever get sick, I want them to pray for me." wow !!!

I chuckled with a big smile I replied, "Isn't he awesome!"

Was it my positive affirmation, was it faith, or was it the prayers in the masses or all of the above? How did I just know she was going to be okay? Was it God's way of strengthening my faith? Whatever it was, it was God's plan, if only to make a believer out of one doctor.

CHAPTER 7
The Dreams Return

In January 2004, I sat straight up in bed. I had been dreaming. I looked at the clock, and it was 5:00 AM. I got up and walked the floor, trying to calm myself, replaying the dream over in my head, scene by scene. Mark was in a car chase. Bullets were flying, as someone lay on top of him as if to protect him. I had this uneasy feeling that what I saw in my dream was happening in real life at the same time I dreamt it.

I didn't go back to sleep. It was the middle of the afternoon in Iraq, and I knew I couldn't get a hold of Mark. Instead, I prayed for his safety and asked God to let me hear from him. Our usual phone time was around 10:30 in the morning, so I had several hours to wait nervously. At 10:40 when the phone rang I was sitting right beside it.

After our "Hello's" I point blank asked him, "Were you involved in an incident this afternoon?" He got very quiet and the minutes ticked on the clock. He never talked much about the things that happened over there, because he didn't want me to worry any more than I already did.

He then answered, "Yes... there was a car chase."

Before he could finish, I replied, "Someone was chasing the car you were in, and I saw you on the floorboard in the back seat, and your PSD (personal security detail) lay on top of you to protect you. Your driver was trying to outrun the gunfire."

Again, silence, tick-tick-tick, when he asked, "How did you know that?"

I answered, "I saw it happen in my dream like a movie playing in my mind."

He knew about some of my experiences in the past, but neither of us understood how I knew things. He then began to explain the events and assured me he was fine. He also admitted that me knowing the details freaked him out.

The fact that I could feel the danger he was in made him uneasy. I had just had a vivid dream, a type of experience that I hadn't had in many years.

I didn't understand this was a form of clairvoyance. My faith tells me; I was shown in my dream what was occurring; I woke up and began to pray and God answered my prayers for his safety.

Bubba comes Home

Mom had always been Bubba's rock. She wrote and visited him faithfully. However, with her health declining the letters and visits had stopped in 2001.

In her place, I began writing him, giving him updates on her, and our family. In our correspondence, over time I began to open my heart and listen. So, for you to better understand my story I am guided to give you a few more details of his.

Dad and Bubba never had a close relationship. When I got married and moved out, they had just begun on the road to building a relationship, a father-son respect, and friendship they had never had, then within three months dad transcended. In the beginning, I knew Bubba was smoking pot, but I thought it was just something he was going through, and he would work it out. I wasn't aware his grief broke him and consumed him until it turned to anger. That angry stage lasted many years and led him to prison.

However, in time through those letters, I saw the brother I grew up with, and my heart opened to him and not that he needed it but I forgave him for putting mom in danger, forgave myself for closing my heart to him. Through those letters, I learned what had changed his life, and why he made the choices he made. I also learned as many in those dark, lonely cells do, he took a hard look at himself and reconnected with Christ. Over the years he had made some positive changes in his life, and I was proud of him and for him. Out of the drug induced state of mind, he was once again the loving friend I knew growing up. He had enrolled in school and graduated college with a two-year degree. He had re-dedicated his heart to God and become an ordained minister.

Now 2004 Bubba was coming up for review with the parole board, working with the same attorney that mom had hired. I picked up the reigns, and found a halfway house in San Antonio that would take him upon his release. Through the halfway house I found him a sponsor. I wrote letters to the parole board members and showed up to testify at his hearing.

On April 4, 2004, Bubba was a free man; he would no longer live out his life behind bars. He was on parole after eleven years and some odd months in prison.

As I think back now, I still tear up. It's nothing like in the movies where you see the family standing outside the gates, and the prisoners walk to the gate, and it opens. For security reasons, we were not allowed anywhere near where the inmates would exit. We had to wait in a waiting area for family and friends about a hundred yards away from the entrance. As Kevin, Adam and I stood there with probably sixty others. I felt anxious, and checked my watch every few minutes, as I stared down the street continually to see those double doors open.

I felt my heart jump when I saw him as he walked amongst the sea of inmates just released. I saw him approaching, and our eyes made contact I read his lips as he looked up and said: "Thank You, Jesus."

My love overflowed at the sight of him. In tears, I heard myself yell, "My Bubba," as I hugged him, we both stood there in tears as we shared a moment of love, gratitude, and joy. I was no longer angry, and my Bubba was back, the little boy I grew up with was back.

It was a five-hour trip back to Canyon Lake, and he talked nonstop. I had arranged with his sponsor that I would take him to the halfway house the next day. Today would be a day of celebration. We stopped and had lunch, bless his heart he ate like he hadn't eaten in years.

Next stop, to visit Mom, I hadn't mentioned that he was getting out, and if I had, she might not remember. Bubba wanted it to be a surprise. Looking back at that day; I walked in first, Bubba much taller than I towered behind me.

Mom looked up, and her eyes brightened, Bubba said, "Hey Gorgeous, what are you doing?"

She smiled and replied, "Waiting for you."

They embraced then she touched his check and wiped a tear that rolled down his face. It was a beautiful, emotional scene of the bond of love between a mother and her child.

Mom's health continued to decline as dementia grew ever more present and her diabetes claimed two of her toes for lack of circulation. In August 2004, I began to get the overwhelming knowing that I needed to spend more time with her. I talked it over with Mark, and in September I called my boss and resigned from the company I had been with for over twenty years.

I had been the constant in mom's life for years now as her health declined. At times, she didn't know who I was, but as the visit went on, she would come back so to speak and remember I was her daughter. I lived for those moments that the metal door was ajar.

Bubba and Kevin visited as often as they could. I knew not seeing the decline in her health and then seeing her now, it must have been hard for them. However, she would always have a few lucid moments until she passed on.

That Christmas I made a collage of family photos and hung it in her room. The nurses would ask mom daily who these people were, most of the time she didn't know, but you could always find her looking at the photos.

I would like to think the pictures of her family gave her peace inside. In the caverns of her mind, she knew those pictures were about home, love, and family; at least I would like to believe so.

Mom had so many imaginary adventures; she would tell the most amazing stories that she believed were true. I never knew what would be going on when I walked in. I had to save her from a man with a knife. Apparently, he wanted to kill her. She saw and heard small children when there were none that we could see. I battled snakes that were either under her bed or crawling up her leg. She was cooking, lying in her bed, or sitting in her chair measuring flour, making biscuits.

One time she flew a helicopter and another the richest man in Texas wanted to marry her, he climbed in her window so she had to have guards posted at her door. She lost her mother's car key's (my grandmother never drove a car, much less owned one.) We had some unbelievable imaginary adventures together. In her mind, we visited so many interesting places, and I would pretend I saw what she was seeing. I was her sister, her mother, her friend, her daughter.

There were other times when I was hit and cursed and told to leave. I chose to be there, and I came to understand that woman who hit and cursed me was not the woman who raised me. I embraced those moments that she was the mother I used to know, no matter how few and far between they were becoming, she was my mom and I loved her.

The doctors had told me that I should correct her when she started talking and thinking she is someplace else or that I was someone else. At first, I tried, but I would see the confusion and the hurt on her face; and I never forgot the words she said to me, "I'm losing my mind. I know it, and there is nothing I can do about it."

Then in time, I decided I wouldn't correct her anymore, and from that day forward I would go with her, wherever her mind led. I would be there with her. I have often wondered if dementia is God's way of hiding the pain our bodies go through as we age with a disease.

Who's to say that the mind can't escape to another place and time, much like the imagination of a child who tells wild tales? Who's to say that they aren't past life memories?

My thought; "It's *so much easier if we just Go Where They Are, rather than fight it!*"

CHAPTER 8
The Mystical Year

The last time our family had been together was Christmas 2004. It had been months since we were all united. Now spring 2005 and the nursing home was hosting a Mother's Day Luncheon on Saturday, May 5. I had this overwhelming knowing that we all needed to be together. I called my brothers and kids; I knew it would be a nice surprise for mom if we were all there. That Saturday afternoon my brothers and I, three grandchildren and the first great-grandchild went to visit mom.

It wasn't one of her best days as we celebrated Mother's Day with her on this beautiful sunny afternoon. She sat in silence, and occasionally I could see a smile in her eyes. She picked at her food, but oh goodness she enjoyed her desert. After lunch we all noticed mom was getting tired, we rolled her back to her room, and we said our goodbyes. We were all thankful to have spent the day together. That day was a beautiful, abundant day, a memory of sharing love and family, one we would all cherish dearly in the future.

I visited mom on Wednesday afternoon, when I walked in I spoke with Mary, the nurse in charge of the shift. She spotted the small banana split, and said, "She doesn't want to eat today. Maybe that will tempt her."

Mom had lost weight due to her periods of not eating; she also had times that she would forget that she ate, and tell me they didn't feed her. Now at 5'8 and 120 lbs it became my habit to bring her something to eat when I came, a meal, soup, salad, or snacks. Sometimes she would eat and sometime she wasn't hungry. When I walked in mom looked over at me, I smiled and asked, "How are you today mom?"

She replied, "Okay." Then she spied the banana split, "I'm waiting on that banana split," she said. Oh yes, she loved sweets, and at the age of 81, I felt she could have what she wanted from time to time. She enjoyed it wholeheartedly, as she told me about a handsome man that came and stayed with her all night the night before.

The following Saturday this feeling crept in that I needed to visit her. I couldn't get her out of my mind. I had planned to go on Sunday, telling myself I would go tomorrow. I ran to the store late afternoon and all the way there and back I kept feeling like I should have gone today. I shook it off and told myself I'll cook a roast and veggies and take her a nice lunch and spend the afternoon with her tomorrow.

It was around 6:00 that evening when the nursing home called to tell me that mom was on her way to the hospital. She had been complaining of stomach pain all day, and when the doctor made his afternoon rounds, he thought it best to have her admitted for a lower GI test. My first thought was *no wonder I had been thinking about her all afternoon.*

I called Kevin and told him I got a call from the nursing home. When I finished relaying the information he said he'd go with me to the hospital. I called Bubba who was at a church function, and he asked that I call him back when I got there and got the information on her condition.

After arriving at the hospital, we were told that it appeared to be a bowel infection.

The doctor explained, "There is no alarm, we've given her something for the pain, and we've started her on an IV of strong antibiotics, she should be okay. I'd like to keep her overnight on the IV and let the antibiotics do their work."

I reported the update to Bubba, then added, "We're going to stay until they get her in a room, then we'll be heading home. They've given her pain meds, so she will probably sleep through the night. I'll come back in the morning and follow the van back to the nursing home and get her settled in."

"Do I need to come?" I couldn't answer that. I repeated what the doctor said, and told him that was up to him. We agreed that the doctor wasn't alarmed, and with the antibiotics she should be feeling better by tomorrow. He decided she needed the rest and he would visit her the following day.

As I sat next to her bed in the emergency room, she asked, "Who's the man standing there?"

"Mom, that's Kevin."

She shook her head. "No not Kevin. That handsome man with the beautiful smile and piercing eyes, he's standing right there." She pointed to the corner of the room.

I thought that she imagined it, I just answered, "I don't know him, mom."

I explained to her that they were going to keep her overnight she nodded to say she understood, as she drifted off to sleep. We sat with her and waited until later that evening when they had space for her.

"Mom they're going to take you to a room now," I said. "You'll stay here tonight, and I'll see you in the morning. Is there anything I can get you before I leave?"

She stared up at me with a twinkle of love in her eyes.

"Mom, is something wrong, are you in pain? What are you staring at?"

Then her smile went from her eyes to her lips, and she answered, "I'm looking at my baby girl. I love you. You know that, don't you?

"Yes Mom, I know that, and I love you."

She continued to stare at me when I saw a tear form, and I reached down to hug her, she whispered in my ear, "I love you, but I am just so tired Dianne." When I rose up she looked into my eyes.

I smiled, as the tears pooled in my eyes, I kissed her, cheek, and I hugged her again, and as I squeezed her hand, I whispered in her ear, "I love you mom. It's okay to go to sleep."

Kevin leaned over and kissed her forehead, "See you in the morning mama. Get some rest, okay." She smiled and patted his hand and said, "I love you."

He replied, "I love you too mama."

They took mom to her room, and again I wondered, *should we stay with her?*

I had an uneasy feeling in the pit of my stomach. But I shook it off, *it's an infection the medicine will kick in she'll feel better*

96

by tomorrow. On our way out; I asked the nurse if they were sure we didn't need to stay with her, "We've started her on the antibiotics they should clear the infection. With the sedative, we've given her, honestly honey, she'll probably sleep all night. She's going to a semiprivate room, so you only have another half hour and visiting hours will be over," the nurse said politely.

Mom was already sleeping and there was nothing we could do so with that information and some hesitation we made the decision to go home for the evening.

Early Sunday morning I was dreaming, I was with mom, and we were laughing about something. It was that hold your belly kind of laugh; then I faintly heard a phone ringing.

"I have to go. You'll need to answer that," she said. I woke up and looked around expecting to find her there. That's how real the dream felt. Then I realized my phone was ringing.

I groggily reached over answering it, "Hello."

"Mrs. Morgan, this is Nurse Sharp I'm your mothers' nurse.

"Yes," I replied. "The Doctor asked me to call you. Your mother had a stroke in her sleep this morning. She is unresponsive. There is fluid building up around her heart. We started her on medication to relieve the fluid, but it's not working."

I sat up in a panic, "What? What does that mean?" My mind was screaming this can't be; she was fine, it was a stomach ache.

"I am afraid that her organs are shutting down. I am calling to ask what you and your family wants us to do? An option would be to put her on life support."

"No," I snapped. "That's not what mom would want. The nursing home has a copy of her DNR, (Do Not Resuscitate Order). Please just stay with her and keep her comfortable, I don't want her to be alone if she goes before I get there. I'm on my way."

"I promise, I will stay here with her," she replied.

Mom and I had many conversations on the subject of how to die. We agreed that when it was God's call, it was time to go. She had a DNR drawn up years ago before the knee surgery and as much as it hurt I was following her wishes. I began to sob, as I realized last night she was telling me goodbye, and that handsome man she visited with and then saw in the corner was an Angel or Jesus waiting to escort her home. Whoever it was I was grateful he had been with her all week. She will no longer be in pain kept entering my mind as I was dressing. Then I thought *I should have stayed with her.*

I called Kevin and Bubba and told them what was going on. I picked Kevin up on the way, but Bubba would meet us there. I flew out the door.

On the way to the hospital, Kevin and I were both in shock as we discussed the conversations of the night before and how she was okay when we left. We both agreed if we had known we would have stayed. I now realize we were both feeling guilty for leaving her, even though it was a stroke and not the infection. We both knew logically that the stroke would have happened where ever she was, but that didn't alleviate the guilt.

As we walked into the hospital, my cell phone rang. "Hello."

"Mrs. Morgan, this is Nurse Sharp, your mom has just passed away. She went very peacefully."

"We're in the lobby and on our way, up."

Our goodbye the night before was sweet. It was closure, and now I feel like she was asking for permission to leave us, she had suffered for many years, and now she was at peace.

On the way home Kevin made the comment "I think she waited for Bubba to come home."

I agreed that mom hung on to see Bubba a free man. Perhaps, she asked God to let her stay long enough to see him living and loving and happy which let her leave with peace.

I have often wondered why mom chose to leave just as we arrived, I even thought as a mom it was her last act of protecting her children from watching her take that final breath, creating an even deeper heartbreak. However, I carried that guilt for not being there to hold her hand when she crossed over, yet deep in my soul I know for reasons unknown I wasn't supposed to be there. Perhaps it was an agreement our hearts made with our Creator long before we arrived on earth.

More importantly, I now realize Spirit was sending a message to me for my entire family to be together on that Saturday afternoon at the nursing home. I am ever so grateful that I received it and paid attention to it. Some would try to argue that it is a gut instinct; I laugh and reply a gut instinct is an intuition, which is a God-given connection to all of us.

Since my awakening, I have had other thoughts on dementia. How do we know the soul doesn't remember past lives? Those of us listening to our loved ones think they are speaking crazily, but perhaps they have experienced the reality they are remembering. They don't know you, because in that reality, that lifetime, you could have been someone else in the soul family, you looked different, had a different name, or were even the opposite sex of who you are now.

Not a scientific or medical explanation, but I've planted the seed for thought.

A Visit with Mom!

A couple of weeks later as I sat on the porch, I started talking out loud to mom. I had never felt my dad's presence around me, but for some reason, I felt like mom was there. I wasn't sure if she could hear me, but I believed she could. While sitting there, I thought I felt a gentle touch across my cheek. I smiled as the tears streamed down my face. I didn't know how I knew, but I just knew it was her. The feeling that she was with me began to happen often. Not sure of what was happening, I didn't tell anyone. I questioned, "Was this truly happening or did I want it to be real so badly that I accepted it as truth." But then I thought *why wouldn't it be natural; I talk to God and hear him/her.*

In June, a neighbor friend by the name of Sandy invited me to a luncheon for a non-profit organization which supported brain related disorders and injuries. Being an issue very dear to my heart I accepted. As I set and listen to the speakers and the work the group had done that year, I knew this was something I would like to be involved with.

I met many beautiful strong women and buried myself in volunteer work. It would be later that I met my first spiritual friend through this group, but not just yet God's plan had to play out before I was ready.

It was now October 2005 when I was looking for something in a drawer; I came across a music box that mom had given me many Christmas's ago. I opened it and read the inscription, "Always my Daughter, now to my Friend." I wound it, sat down on the side of the bed and smiled as I listened to the beautiful soft melody. I said, "Oh mom I miss you so much."

Then I felt her presence, just a knowing that she was there, and as the sweet music began to fill the room, I heard her say, "I'm right here."

"I know you're always with me," I answered.

"No, I'm right here honey."

I was the only one in the house, I looked around the room. "Hello," I yelled.

I heard her laugh and then she said, "I can hear you. You don't have to yell."

"Mom" I whispered, then I asked, "Mom is that you?"

"Yes, I've never left you baby girl you just can't see me. But through your gift, you have been feeling my energy, and you can hear me in your thoughts."

"That was you, that I felt touch my cheek!"

"Yes."

"I knew it!" Then I began to cry when I felt a soft, gentle touch go across my cheek.

Whatever it was, I was excited to know I had felt mom's presence! I hadn't yet understood that thinking of something she might say, or to hear her favorite song was one of the ways she connected with me. Now I heard her voice but not her voice outside my head, her voice was coming inside my head.

In my excitement, I called Danielle, Anne, and Adam to tell them what had just happened. Not sure if they believed me or not, I had to share this joy!

They all listened, they didn't doubt me, but I felt they didn't understand it all, but that was okay I didn't either!

Within the next week I got a call from Danielle.

"Mom the oddest thing just happened."

"What's that?" I asked.

"I was lying across my bed and talking to Grandma's picture that sits on the dresser. I was crying and telling her how much I missed her. Mom, her picture fell off the dresser. I sat it back up thinking *that was odd* and it fell over again!"

I laughed and answered, "I think you just had visit from your grandma, and she wanted you to know she was there with you, so she knocked the picture over to get your attention."

That same week Anne called to tell me about a dream she had.

"Grandma was in my dream last night. Mom it felt so real, like she was really with me."

We were having our own visits from mom in different ways that would resonate with each of us. If Adam had a visit he didn't share it, but that was okay it was his to cherish.

Mom would send me little signs through songs, sayings, smells, the first being that music box. There were times when I felt her and heard her voice, other's it was inside my head; or I smelt Juicy Fruit Gum, her favorite. One night I was depressed and speaking to her, I felt her arms wrap around me for comfort. I was never frightened when she visited; I was thankful I still had her and something deep inside of me felt it was normal long before I realized it was!

On one of Mark's two week leaves at home he walked in on me having a conversation with her.

The words came out before I thought them, "I was talking to mom."

You have heard the expression "priceless" well that was the look on his face.

I began to explain, "I have been hearing her for a while now, and she's visited the girls as well."

In that skeptical deep voice of his, he replied, "Okaaay."

In my matter of fact manner, I answered him, "I believe and if you believe then anything is possible. Having conversations with her gives me comfort, so if I'm crazy so be it. At least I am happy."

Of course, being a man of logic, he was trying to find it, where there was none, other than this was one of my stages of grief or I really was going crazy and had pulled the girls into it. When I saw that look on his face I then reminded him of a conversation we had many years back.

I asked, "Do you remember in the 90's, and we were watching a Psychic-Medium program on television, and you asked, 'Do you think he can do that, do you think it's real?"

He answered, "Not really, maybe."

"Without hesitation, I answered you, 'My answer would be yes. Why wouldn't we be able to talk to the other side? I talk to God, and everything in me knows I hear him so why not? In fact I wish I could.'"

He didn't know how to respond to that. "Okay, but do you really hear her?" He asked.

"I really don't know how to explain it, I do but I don't. Sometimes I hear her voice, but most of the time I just know it's her from the feeling and the thoughts that pop in my head when I ask her a question."

He gave me the strangest look and we didn't talk about it again for several years.

Now I think perhaps at the time, I made that statement to Mark, "I wish I could do that." I once again set my free will into motion, and God and the Universe said: "In time my child!"

CHAPTER 9
Bubba's Story

As mentioned previously Bubba had become an ordained minister while incarcerated. Through letters with a fellow Christian inmate, he learned of a non-denominational church in San Antonio. In summer of 2004 he called and spoke with Pastor Jim, who soon became his mentor. Through the churches guidance Bubba left the half-way house and got an apartment. He then started his own business as a house painter and the members of the church supplied him with clients. This was a good transition for him and he became very involved with his new church family. Bubba also met and married a young woman from the church named Becka in March 2005. Mom did get to see he had made a happy life for himself. He told me once, "I have Jesus in my heart, a loving wife, a motorcycle, and my dog. Life is good."

While in prison Bubba had been diagnosed with Hepatitis C so other than his health problems he was doing well until summer of 2005 when he had been in an auto accident which resulted in numerous surgeries. After that, he had rods in his knees and back, and they were very bothersome. However; with his past addiction to drugs, he chose to deal with the pain without pain management. He had also gained about 80 lb.'s since his release from prison, which the extra weight made the pain worse. After one of his doctor's appointments, I asked, "What'd the doctor say?"

His reply, "I'm fine, blood pressure is high, I need to lose some weight. There's a new medication he wants me to try for the Hep C, but it's too expensive, and without insurance, I can't afford it. He gave me a blood pressure medication and told me to continue my Hep C medication."

I somehow knew he wasn't telling me the whole story. I just had the feeling the news the doctor had given him was not good, and he didn't want to worry me.

It was a few weeks after this conversation I was having a get together at my home and invited Bubba and Becka. I wanted to introduce them to a couple that I had met. I commented, "I think you'll like Fran and Bill, they're a religious couple, so you'll have a lot in common."

His sea blue eyes so full of light smiled down at me (he was my baby brother at 6'2" and 295lb's, I'm 5'3) I wasn't expecting the response he gave, "That's sweet of you Dianne, but I'm not religious, I am spiritual."

I smiled as I didn't know how to answer him. I thought if one went to church, and were part of an organized religion and talked about God and Jesus as he did, well then they were religious. Spiritual was a new term, a new direction that I hadn't explored.

One afternoon in spring 2006 Bubba called, the excitement in his voice was at an all time high. "Hey kiddo, (his term of endearment for the women in his life) I just wanted to invite you to church this Sunday."

I was a little hesitant which he picked up on and then continued, "I'm going to be speaking."

"Really," I said.

"Yes. The pastor has asked me to tell my story of finding Jesus. They want me to ride in the auditorium on my motorcycle. They're going to have the news footage of my arrest playing on a big screen as I ride in."

Even though I was hesitant, I replied, "Of course. I wouldn't miss it."

On Sunday morning, I drove the hour and a half drive to the church in San Antonio. They had a special place for me to sit with Becka and close friends. Strangers came up to introduce themselves to me and take a minute to tell me what a blessing Bubba had been to the church. My heart was full; and I was so proud of him and happy he had found his place, his peace.

I was thinking *how wonderful God is* when the big screen at the front of the auditorium came on and there in front of me was an angry, lost man looking out at the crowd. His long blonde hair and his hollow sea blue eyes, this was my brother in 1992. I had never seen the news footage, and I cried as I watched it. Mom had described it correctly; there was Bubba handcuffed and thrown in the police car; he glanced back over his shoulder and with such hatred as he spit at the camera. As they panned the yard, I saw my mom escorted to the back of another police car and Bubba's dog Fishie lying in a pool of blood. The newscaster was saying something about a year long drug investigation came to an end at the North Houston Home of "Bubba" Phillips today.

After the news report had shown the raid and his arrest the screen went blank, and a loud roar came from the back of the church. It was Bubba starting up his Harley and riding up the aisle.

He told the congregation the story of his life. He choked up several times as he spoke "I was mad at God when our father died, and I blamed God. I rebelled against God."

As he told his story, I cried for his pain. As I mentioned we never talked about our feelings, so I never knew any of this. I never knew how my brother felt, but do we truly know another's heart? He explained that he was never angry about my relationship with dad, but he longed for one of his own. I knew Bubba began to change after dad died, there were signs, but I was too wrapped up in my own life to see them. When Andrew and I moved in he wasn't home much, and when he was we didn't talk feelings, so I had no idea the storm he was battling.

Bubba was classified as a racist in prison and put in solitary confinement for many years. He began to tell the story of a trustee, a man of color named Pat that brought his food. He started to cry when he spoke, "For over two years I was so hateful to him, I spat on him and called him awful names every day. Then one Thanksgiving when he brought me my food tray and I told him to bring me another helping. You should understand that Turkey and dressing dinner was like a T-bone steak. Pat said, 'you know I can't do that.' I cussed him out."

Bubba swallowed and cleared his throat. "A few minutes later the metal food door opened again, and there was a second tray. I asked him, 'Why'd you bring me this?'" Bubba was crying again, and through the sobs, he explained, "He said 15 words that changed my life, "God put it on my heart to bring it to you, because he loves you."

"As I sat there and ate my turkey dinner I began to ask, why would God love me after all I've done. How could he love me, after the hatred I have shown him? I began to cry, I was so ashamed, and the next thing that happened was my miracle. Through my sobbing, God spoke to me. I released all my anger, all my hurt as I asked God for forgiveness'. I felt a warm embrace, and at that moment I knew his mercy, his love. Wrapped in his grace, I was no longer angry with God. I had hurt so many people in my life as I headed down the road of self-destruction not caring who I took with me. I prayed that night, the first time I had prayed in years. The next day I asked Pat if he could bring me a Bible. Pat now my brother in Christ, became one of my best friends in the remaining years of my incarceration."

Then Bubba said something that I had thought many times, "If I hadn't ended up in jail I wouldn't be standing here talking to you today. It was all part of God's plan." He stopped and dried his eyes then he pointed at me and said, "If it weren't for my sister sitting over there, my mom and my grandma who have already returned home to heaven, I would have died long before I went to prison. They didn't give up on me, and in prison, I discovered Jesus didn't give up on me either."

There wasn't a dry eye in the house, including mine, as he told his story of getting reacquainted with God, and Jesus.

Later that afternoon Bubba and I sat on his patio talking. I felt it was time for me to tell him I could communicate with mom. I hadn't told him, I think partly because he always thought I was weird but also because he might judge that it was a sin; but at this moment I somehow knew he would believe me. I said, "I'm going to share something with you that you might find hard to understand."

He said, "Okay, try me."

I answered, "I have been talking to mom on the other side for a while now. I can feel her here with us. But not only do I feel her presence, I hear her. Not like her standing there talking to me, but in my mind."

His response was a smile that came as love deep from the soul, and said, "I haven't told anyone this part of my story. That night in that dark cell when I asked God how could you love me? I said, God spoke to me, I mean I heard him audibly say, 'Because you are my child!' I didn't doubt that I heard God's voice, and if I can hear him, why couldn't you hear mom? "' Then he hugged me and jokingly added, "You've always been weird."

It was a good day, a healing day, as I finally got the answers to the questions I never asked and shared my gift with Bubba who also had gifts to share. Funny, how we share some bits of our life and refrain from telling all in the fear of being judged.

A few months had gone by it was now the end of September 2006. Summer was hanging on, and it was a warm afternoon when the phone rang. Caller ID told me it was Bubba.

I answered, "Hey there, what's up?

Once again there was an overwhelming excitement in his voice. "Hey, I just had to share this with you. You knew they recorded my sermon on DVD?"

"Yes, I'd still like to get a copy of it for the kids."

"Okay, I'll get you one, but I have to tell you something. That Sunday, there were visitors at the church from Germany. God touched them through my words. They loved it so much they bought a dozen copies of the DVD to take back to share with their church, and families that had loved ones in prison."

"Wow! That is awesome Bubba!"

"Yep! The law of man says I can't leave Texas. God is sending me around the world to share his message!"

Oh, what a blessing this was for him. God was at work in his life, and he so deserved this joy. Bubba was a decent man who once upon a time lost his way. Through some very rough times, he found his way back to the light and was shining it so bright for others to see. He shows others through his walk with Christ, how God works in our lives when we invite him in.

October 10, 2007

The Accident

2007 went rapidly, and fall was approaching. I had a limestone back yard with very little grass and Bubba and I had on ongoing joke. When I would say I need to mow he kidded me that I mowed my dirt! I decided I'd show him. I was researching sods that would grow in this limestone ground. A dear friend came to help me and we worked for a full weekend, I finished on Tuesday, and I watered real grass not just dirt and weeds. I was pretty proud of myself, four long days of work yet I now had grass to mow instead of dirt! I chuckled as I thought of Bubba.

Bubba had been on my mind all day. I knew he went to Houston to visit an old friend. He would call me when he got home. I started to call him a couple of times that day but decided it was silly, and I was over protective. *I'll call him tomorrow to invite him to come see my yard this weekend."* I thought.

At 2:00 AM in the morning the following day, the phone woke me. I could barely make out the voice through the crying. "Dianne," my sister-in-law Becka said.

"Yes, what's wrong?"

"Bubba was in a motorcycle accident in Houston. He's unconscious. I'm on my way there."

"Are you driving?" I sat up on the side of the bed and listened.

"No, Pastor Jim is taking me. I don't know anything, except he had a wreck and they took him to the hospital, and he's unconscious."

A wave of heaviness rolled over me. I had a bad feeling, I knew the outcome.

Becka said, "I'll call you when I get there and talk to the doctors."

"Okay honey, call me and let me know what's going on."

I couldn't go back to sleep. I kept thinking, *why didn't I call Bubba yesterday?* I somehow knew I wasn't going to see him again. He wasn't going to wake up. I began to cry as I prayed to God, and then I called to mom, she didn't answer me. I resided in myself she was with Bubba. Next I wondered how I would tell my children.

I called Kevin around 5:00 AM and explained what was going on. He asked me to keep him posted. When Adam got up at 6:30 AM I told him what had happened, he left for work in a daze.

Then I called my girls in Houston around 7:00 AM. They both said they were going to the hospital. Becka called around 7:30 AM. The news wasn't good!

"Bubba still hasn't woken up. He's in a coma." I listened as she explained the head trauma he incurred and the surgery about to be done, as soon as she signed the paperwork. She asked, "Should I let them operate?"

They had taken Bubba to the number one trauma center in Houston. I knew he was in good hands. I gave her the best advice I could. I told her I trusted the doctors there. They knew what was best and to let them do their job.

My daughters checked in with me throughout the morning, his condition wasn't improving. I wanted to go, but I wasn't in any shape to drive. Becka's call came that afternoon, and the news wasn't positive; the doctors had gone in and inserted a tube to release the pressure in his brain. When the surgeons went in to remove his spleen, they discovered his liver was in very grave condition. The doctor reported to Becka that 'IF' he makes it, he would have a rough road ahead."

When I heard those words, I somehow knew what was next. I called Kevin and updated him. I told him I was planning to go to Houston the next day. He said he couldn't get off work and asked that I call him once I got there. I booked a flight for Adam and me for the following morning.

As I sat on the plane I felt my baby brother around me I knew he was leaving us. When we landed in Houston, my cell phone rang. "Mom," Anne said in the softest voice of grief.

"We just landed we'll be out in a minute," I answered.

Through her tears she repeated, "Mom."

"Yes, honey." I knew what she was about to say.

"Uncle Bubba didn't make it; he passed away."

"I know honey; we'll be out front in a minute."

The ride to the hospital was solemn as Anne told me Danielle was there with Becka and Pastor Jim along with a few of Bubba's friends that he had been with when the accident happened. She had gone in and seen him before she came to the airport.

Inside I was broken again, but I couldn't let my babies see it.

I felt all eyes on me when I walked in; as soon as they saw me, Danielle and Becka fell apart. We embraced in tears. Everyone had gone in to see him by the time I got to the hospital. I looked around at the group; Becka, Danielle, Anne, Adam, and Bubba's friends, who all had tears of great sadness running down their faces. *I can't cry, I can't fall apart; stay strong, they all need you, I can do this, don't break down, don't break down.* All of these thoughts were ranting in my mind as I was in a state of shock.

I honestly don't remember if I went into Bubba's room by myself or if others were with me. I stood against the wall for a few minutes just staring at him; this was a dream, it had to be a dream. I felt like he was there watching me, I felt his spirit, his love. I slowly walked over to his lifeless body and looked down at my baby brother. A tear rolled down my cheek as I leaned over and kissed his forehead and whispered: "I love you, Bubba."

I felt compelled to be strong while everyone around me was falling apart. I had to be strong. It hadn't been but a few short months since mom left us and now Bubba! I took responsibility that my children needed me to show strength. The tragedy shook us all to our core.

The next few days were filled with making funeral arrangements, then flying back home. Adam and I picked up Kevin a few days later and drove back to Houston for the service.

On the drive, we were each telling stories of Bubba's humor and quick wit. We laughed so hard and then we all got quiet.

To break the silence I commented, "This could have been so much worse, we could be making this drive to Huntsville. I am grateful that he found peace and happiness and died outside of those prison walls. He died doing something that he loved, riding that dang motor-cicle."

Once the funeral was over, we had dinner with family and a few close friends. It was a quiet three and half hour drive back to Canyon Lake. We arrived home after 11:00 pm.

When we got unloaded, I slumped down on the couch and gazed off, not really looking at anything, but thinking of everything.

Adam noticed I had checked out and he asked, "Are you okay mom?"

With a slight smile I answered, "I'm good honey; I'm just tired."

"Do you mind if I leave you for a while, I need to get some air."

"That's fine. You go on."

We all deal with grief differently and he needed to be away from me so that he could breathe. As he pulled out of the driveway, I shut the door. I waited just long enough until he was out of sight. Then I let out a long huge scream. I threw myself down on the couch and kicked and screamed at God. I threw a tantrum!

"Why?" I yelled.

"Why did you give me my brother back after so many years just to take him away?"

"Why so soon after my Mom, whyyyyyyyyyyyyyy?" I screamed at the top of my lungs.

"I don't understand, and God I am angry," I cried, "it hurts so badly!"

I kept screaming until my throat was hoarse. "Why, why did you take Bubba, I don't understand why him, after all, he's been through why now? God, I am mad."

Then through my tears, I began sobbing out loud to Bubba, "I am sorry I didn't spend time with you lately. You were a pain in my butt, but I loved you so much. Bubba, I'm so sorry I didn't spend more time with you." Then I held my stomach and screamed and cried as I rocked back and forth.

116

It's funny how we believe that we have all the time in the world when everything can change in the blink of an eye. Yes, I was MAD, I lost him years ago when he went to prison, and I finally got my brother back, but now I lost him forever.

I cried and rocked myself to sleep that night, feeling lost, feeling the anger and feeling so sad. My heart hurt.

I got up the next morning and stumbled down the stairs to get coffee. I felt very empty. I can only describe it as a part of me was missing. As I sat outside and sipped my coffee and smoked a cigarette, I looked around at the beauty of that silly green lawn. I cried out. "You'll never get to see my grass."

I leaned back in the chair and closed my eyes, a flash went through my mind of the white light, and the hand offered to me years ago. Remembering having that choice myself, it was at that moment everything in me knew God didn't take my baby brother. My little brother chose to go home.

The next scene flashed through my mind was mom and her last words to me. She had grown weary of the pain of the physical body. She chose to go to her eternal home. Again at that moment I understood death is part of our journey, the graduation if you will. How beautiful it would be if we all understood that death is not the end; that our soul lives on in the Spiritual Realm. That we indeed choose how and when, if only we all understood that, then there would be no fear of death.

Yes, those of us left here would still mourn the loss of no longer physically seeing, hearing or touching that person, but yet all of mankind would rejoice in the knowing of an eternity of pure love. My thoughts were filled with peace as I somehow understood death is a part of life, a transition of rebirth.

Perhaps Bubba couldn't take the pain any longer and when the hand was offered, his love for Jesus was stronger than his will to stay here on earth. I began to cry to God, except this time, I cried an apology for getting so angry with him.

I wiped my tears and sat there as I sipped my coffee, when I heard a familiar voice, "Hey kiddo." Now tears of joy were flowing from my heart.

"Bubba!" I exclaimed, in excitement and in my mind, I could see him smiling.

He laughed, "I somehow knew you'd hear me. Dianne, it is so wonderful here! We become light, it is incredible."

I joyfully talked to him a few minutes, he thanked me for the as he put it 'unusual eulogy.' He reminded me that I am so loved here and there, he wanted me to know he was okay and then his voice began to fade off and I heard him uttered something about one visit at a time. "Bubba, are you still here?" I didn't get a reply, he was gone.

I could hear him, I just didn't understand how. I didn't question it. I just went with it and found comfort in knowing he was still with me.

This is what I was experiencing, and everything in me knew it was real, I didn't imagine it. Nor did I question it.

These are merely some of the reflections of my past, playing them out in my mind and on paper was simply a way to discover the synchronicities in my life and my connection.

Was I always paying attention to the signs? My answers would be, "No!"

I wasn't even aware that these were signs or connections. I couldn't explain any of it, as it was all part of my journey and in time awakened me to my connection with Spirit.

Some of you have had similar experiences in your lives, or know someone that has. What I feel is fascinating, are the many synchronicities in our lives; some would say just a coincidence, odd, strange. Synchronicities are amazing, and they are God's work to get our attention that there is something far greater in control than our own lives.

The Synchronicities of God are here to prompt us to look deeper and not just accept at face value.

This knowing that I didn't know I had, that we all have. I didn't know this type of relationship existed in this way. Even though I was awestruck, I accepted, and it wouldn't be long until I found out how connected we are. I was about to discover a whole new world in the Spiritual Realm.

PART II

Awareness

CHAPTER 10
My Journey to Awareness

You've heard the term, Spiritual Journey. What exactly does that mean? To me, it means a journey that starts from one point with events that lead you to a destination. My Spiritual Journey led me to be aware of my Connection to the Spiritual Realm with my higher self, heart, and soul. It for me was connecting with my Christ Consciousness to Creator. Archangel Chamuel is known as "The Finding Angel," he tells us that everything we are searching for is inside us. It came to me that what he is saying is, everything we are looking for, total peace, love, happiness, joy, and acceptance, is obtainable through our Connection to Creator in our hearts.

Part two, Awareness chapters ten through thirteen I am discovering and accepting my Mystical beliefs. There were many events during this period of my life. I have chosen the few that I felt were significant to my inner path. 2008 thru 2012 was what I feel was the second part of my awakening; with mom transcending in 2005 when my awareness of the connection started. I did not wake up one day and say "I Am on my Spiritual Journey. I Am a Spiritual Being. I Am Connected and I know my Life Purpose and my Divine Life Mission."

This was a deep quest of discovery and exploring. It didn't happen overnight. It's a unique path for each one of us. Once I became aware of my connection with the spiritual realm, I wanted all the answers immediately. Of course, this didn't happen either! As Archangel Michael once told me, "You can't get from zero to God at 60 mph the human body would implode." Hence it is a journey.

I have discovered we live in a world of the impatient reality. I have often thought we have all come in this lifetime to learn patience. Think about it; we want instant gratification. Here in the US we have grown up in a world where all is instantaneous, and we don't have to wait on things we feel we have to have now. Fast food, we can get a meal already made anytime we want it. Credit Cards, we no longer have to save our money for something we want. Cell Phones, a way of portable communication, we can talk to anyone, anytime, anywhere we are.

I now understand that if the journey occurred instantaneously, you would miss out on so many ah-ha moments and being in complete amazement and awestruck at the synchronicities of God. I realize also that many call it woo-woo and that's okay too, because I can tell you, the experience and excitement of woo-woo is utterly mind boggling! The journey we hear so much about is exciting. I believe the journey never ends as we discover more about ourselves, God's Love and Universal Spiritual Law.

Awareness is the understanding of our Connection with the spiritual realm; and to my amazement I was about to become a self-taught explorer.

We've heard that each person goes through bereavement in their own time and way. Some people never get over the loss of a loved one, and others it takes many years. For me, it was from October 2007, and it lasted thirty months or two and a half years.

Those years seemed to fold into one, and I went into a deep depression. I lost myself during that period. I did not know who I was anymore. I felt alone and abandoned!

After Bubba transcended I felt my identity, my roots were gone. I made the statement "I am a fifty-year-old orphan." I loved Kevin and Brenda dearly they were my siblings, but some part of me had left.

Mark was still working overseas, and the kids were grown and out of the house. So here I was on my own so to speak. As time went by I went through the motions of the day to day, walking in a fog. Even though I had a loving family, I tumbled into a dark sea of depression. Not knowing the ego was feeding that broken, buried place of abandonment, as it knocked down and tossed my emotions. The communication with mom and Bubba were my life preservers.

The loss of Bubba hit me hard, and I found comfort in talking to them as it helped keep me from tumbling over the edge and drowning in that depression. I somehow felt I hadn't lost them. I couldn't physically see my loved ones, but I could communicate with them in my mind. No, it wasn't a non-stop conversation, they would drop by so to speak and I always somehow knew when they were there.

There were times I would experience a temperature change in the room and get a chill, and other times I felt the heat around me. I would hear my name called when I was alone. I would see beautiful creamy lights twinkling around me out of the corner of my eye. I saw them dart across the room in front of me. I felt this was normal! I didn't logically understand it, and sometimes I doubted myself, and I thought I imagined the experience. But somehow, I knew it was real. God had given me communication with them, and I was grateful. Was this God's Grace to help me get through the depression? Was it shock? I was still trying to make sense out of it.

Mark wasn't there when Bubba transcended, and he hadn't experienced my steps of grief. So, I suppose not seeing the progression and coming home a few months later was a little disturbing to him. He found me carrying on conversations with what he thought was my mom. When I told him, I was now talking to Bubba too, he was dumbfounded.

He finally told me one day, "You're freaking me out with all this talking to your deceased family."

I admitted to him, "Talking to them brings me comfort." Mark seemed to understand that, however being a daily occurrence as to not 'freak him out,' I agreed to talk to them silently.

When I spoke of talking to mom or Bubba and hearing them to close friends, I got looks of concern. I think they thought this was part of my depression or that I wasn't in touch with reality. I didn't dare tell them of the other events I was experiencing.

2008 – 2011

In January 2008, we were at a restaurant with friends and family for my birthday dinner. Adam was away at school, but both Danielle and Anne had come from Houston for the celebration. While we were waiting for our food, Danielle took my grandson Dante to the restroom.

She came back and whispered, "Mom you're not going to believe this. Dante told me "we have to hurry so I can see Uncle Bubba.' I said Dante, Uncle Bubba's not here.'"

He looked up and said, "Yes he is."

I asked him, "Where."

He said, "He's sitting next to Nana."

I smiled, and in my matter of fact character replied, "Of course where else would he be on my birthday!"

The next morning three-year-old Dante stood at the end of the staircase looking up speaking to someone. When Danielle asked him, "Who are you talking to?"

He innocently but matter-of-factly answered, "Uncle Bubba."

As time went by this became a rather ordinary occurrence.

Dante was born ten months before Bubba transcended, he didn't know his great uncle, and had only been around him a few times. Bubba was visiting with him. The visits were to me another confirmation that what I was experiencing was ever so real.

On one occasion Danielle called, "Mom the freakiest thing happened. Dante was playing and very chatty. I asked him, 'who are you talking to?' Of course, I knew he was going to say Uncle Bubba.'"

I smiled and said, "uh huh."

She continued, "Then I asked him, what's Uncle Bubba doing? Mom, you'll never guess what he said."

I replied, "What honey."

She said, "He said Uncle Bubba was riding his motor-cycle. Mom I have never said that to him!"

I laughed and replied, "That was your confirmation that it is indeed your Uncle Bubba,"

"Mom this is not funny, it's getting weird."

"Y'all may not believe it, but honey I know Bubba and grandma are with us. I've told you I talk to them. Dante is talking to Bubba, and you can speak to him too. From what I have read children under seven see, feel and hear Spirit, and our society hasn't corrected them by telling them it is not real. In other countries and cultures, it is completely natural, and children learn from an early age that our loved ones are very present. They're encouraged to communicate with them. I don't know why here, in this country, we aren't taught that we can communicate with them. Was it intentionally withheld from us that it is real? Perhaps it was left out of religious doctrine and beliefs out of fear that we would talk to the devil?"

We both laughed.

"Maybe it's the fear of judgment from others. I know I get some strange responses when mentioning that I talk to your grandma and Bubba. I don't know honey. Your grandma always told me I had a gift most wouldn't understand. I don't' think she knew what or how to teach me."

Hearing Dante's experiences was another confirmation of my belief that life is never ending, even after death.

Danielle was awakening and finding it hard to believe; she was still in Ah. I was certainly no expert on the subject. I explained the best way I knew how.

After Bubba had departed physically I was still involved with the non-profit for prevention of traumatic brain injuries; it was now in April of 2008, a group of us had gone to Abilene for an annual convention. There were two new members of our local organization with us that I hadn't yet got to know, so the first evening I invited them to meet some of us on the patio for a glass of wine. We sat around and talked and laughed most of the evening.

One of these women by the name of Ginger was a fifty-eight-year-old adorable little woman. I just loved her feistiness; she was unique with her mysterious yet eclectic style, this 5-foot petite, frosted pixie haircut woman with the warmest green eyes was a hoot. I read her as sweet, yet a little mischievous. I now understand I was drawn to her energy, that instantaneous affability when you meet someone, and you instantly feel a connection. Someone you'd like to get to know better. God's plan was in motion and she would become my sister of the heart, my first spiritual friend and teacher, a very important role in my awakening process down the road.

The next evening Ginger and I ended up sitting next to each other at dinner. We discovered we had a lot in common, even quirky things like foods: Fritos mixed with chocolate ice cream. She said something to me that I had never heard before, "I was in the pool earlier, and you walked through the atrium, you may find this odd, but you have the most beautiful aura around you."

I politely answered, "No-one has ever said that to me, thank you." When my actual thought was what the heck is an aura? At the time, I was unaware of the metaphysical world.

Through the evening we were somehow pulled together into understanding and friendship.

Our group schedule included breakfast, and a short goodbye ceremony at 7:00 AM the following morning, and I noticed she wasn't there. It wasn't mandatory to attend, but I found it odd. At 9:30 AM I was back in my room packing when one of the ladies knocked on my door.

When I answered, I could see she was upset then she said, "Ginger received a phone call this morning that her husband had a heart attack and died sometime yesterday evening. They found him in the garage this morning."

Introduced to the Metaphysical

God brings people together at certain times in their lives, for certain reasons and lessons.

After her husband, had transcended, I visited Ginger, and offered her support in any way that she needed, some days it was just to pull her back up out of the rabbit hole. She would enter my thoughts at the oddest times, which would prompt me to call and check on her.

With Mark being gone three months at a time, she and I spent many hours together. Through her healing process and my recent losses, we had our emotional similarities; grief, loss, and coping.

I told her the story of my brother's visits to my grandson. Reassured her loved ones are always with us. She was open to my stories and very accepting of my beliefs. That led us to many more spiritual conversations in which I told her I hear mom and Bubba. She didn't judge me, in fact she too heard the spiritual realm!

From 2009-2011 Ginger and I became very close friends. Puzzling that somehow, we had similar beliefs on the Spiritual Realm when she grew up in a world that practiced metaphysics and spirituality, and I grew up in a family with Christian evangelistic beliefs. She knew Jesus as an Ascended Master (a new term for me), and I knew him as the son of God, and part of me felt he was the physical incarnation of God. Some of our beliefs were similar, and we found common ground on others. I didn't thoroughly agree with everything she said, nor did she agree with me. However, something was going on with me, and perhaps with her help, I could find answers. I was having conversations with my mom and my brother, and recently I had thought I heard other voices!

During those three years, she answered many questions for me and introduced me to many spiritual tools. One day she mentioned Archangel Michael. Who was he? I was intrigued and wanted to understand this new-found world.

She introduced me to oracle cards with a deck of Archangel Michael cards and explained them to me. Oh! Oracle Card Readings was something I had never heard of, something new! I surprised her one afternoon when I said, "I ordered a set of Archangel Michael Cards. I don't know how to use them will you teach me?"

I worked with the Archangel Michael cards daily and I was building a relationship with him! For unknown reasons, I felt close to him, I trusted him. I was amazed at the accuracy of the messages I received. I now understand that Oracle cards work through the law of attraction.

Ginger bought me my first pendulum for Christmas in 2010 and taught me how to use it. She introduced me to meditation. Ginger also loved crystals, and I began to ask questions. How do they work; which led me to purchase my first stone of clear quartz. Through the years she introduced me to Tarot cards, which I can honestly say I didn't find as thrilling as Michael, I didn't resonate with them. We discussed many spiritual topics, including the battle of light and dark of the spiritual realm. As I began to understand the spiritual realm it led to more questions and many hours of conversations between the two of us.

In our conversations Ginger and I would both hear the spiritual realm and laugh then compare what we heard, asking each other, "What did you hear?" I don't think at the time that I understood this was exercising my psych abilities and that I did hear spirit loud and clear. God Always has a PLAN!

CHAPTER 11
2012 The Year of Change!

By this time there was a lot of chatter on the internet about the December 2012, which revolved around the Mayan Calendar. Many thought the world was coming to an end, and many related that date with the beginning of a new golden age of consciousness and prosperity. My guides have since explained this was the shift into Christ Consciousness for each of us on earth. Hence it was the end of the world as we knew it as more souls would be awakening to their connection with the spiritual realm.

Again, questions answered led to more questions.

I also went through many shifts that year. I knew I heard the spiritual realm, but there was a desire in me, driving me forward to explore metaphysics and spirituality even deeper. Why did I have the need to understand it? I became fascinated with magic. At the time I had yet to discover we all hold Divine Magic within us. Through my studies I understood that the term "Witch" was given to practitioners or seers to describe something not understood.

I also understood there is light and dark in everything. The outcome is the intention that you put into the practice. I began to write incantations and performed simple ceremonies. I understood that everything you put out into the universe returns to you. I wished no harm to anyone.

I was still working with the Archangel Michael Oracle Cards and searching for answers to my path. Ginger could only explain what I was going through as, "You are experiencing rapid understanding and spiritual growth."

For the Love of Adam

Adam was now twenty-eight, over the years he continually went through hard times. I didn't understand it; he would appear to be doing fine. He'd get a new job and begin to move forward for a period, then out of nowhere he would slide back down into his old patterns. As most parents do, I worried about him. In my heart I knew he was a good man, he had a good heart. Not just because he was my son, but because of the kindness, compassion, and love he showed others.

I questioned, "What is blocking him from achieving his goals and living a successful, happy life?"

Now he was once again going through a rough patch. Apparently, he over slept and didn't call in until late afternoon and lost yet another job. I honestly did not understand the pattern.

He and I talked daily. We discussed many things the metaphysical being one of them. He found it odd when I began to talk about crystals and spells.

I asked, "Are you laughing at me?"

"No mom it just sounds strange to hear you talk about things that some of my friends are into."

Through this particular conversation, I told him I had been reading about magic.

He asked, "So are you studying Wicca? I have friends that are Wiccan." I answered, "Not exactly. I would like to try and help you move forward. I have a feeling that someone has

134

surrounded you with negative energy. I want to try to return it where it came from, but I think I need your permission."

His answer was, "Of course mom, do what you need to do. I know you wouldn't hurt me, I trust you."

Later that week was Full Moon it felt right to perform the ceremony at that time. Ginger and I held the return to others spell, burning candles repeating an incantation to send the negative energy surrounding him back to where it originated. Things did improve for him. Wow, this was real, and I could do this!

However, within months the cycle reoccurred, and Adam had lost yet another job. I just couldn't understand how he could keep going backward. It broke my heart when he said, "Why does this keep happening to me, Mom?"

The next morning after one of these conversations I expressed my concerns to Ginger. "It seemed the incantation worked for a while but then here we go again. He just can't move forward in life. I feel he may give up and head down a path of self-destruction. He's so depressed; I don't know what to do?"

I was expressing my feelings and genuinely wanted advice when I asked Ginger to help me figure out what this was all about. "Do you think he has an entity attached to him?" Ginger asked.

"I don't know, how would I know that?"

"You talk to Bubba, ask him?"

I closed my eyes, and concentrated on my brother, "Bubba is there an entity attached to Adam?" I waited for his reply.

Immediately I heard him say "Yes."

"What do I do?" I asked.

I heard Bubba faintly say something about guidance and then I started crying, feeling what I would best describe as lost.

I had to digest this, and figure out what this entity was and why was it attached to my child! I felt anger building up inside of me. I was going to save my son no matter what the cost was. I just needed to know what to do and who I was dealing with!

I began to search the web for information on entities and to ask Ginger questions since she had more knowledge on attachments than I had. Was this for real? I thought it was only in the movies and books. Now I had just discovered this was true, that there are souls who do not go to the light and attach to others for many different reasons. The idea was mind blowing!

Ginger suggested, "This is just a thought, but you talk to your Mom and Bubba, and yet you've never talked to your Dad. Have you ever wondered why? It could be him who has attached to your son."

Over the next few days, I began to pray for direction and answers. I loved my Dad, but I have to tell you I had mixed emotions. I was sad, but it also made me furious at him.

I yelled at him, "You've lived your life, why do you want to live it through my son now." I would sit and talk to him, hollering at him for staying and not going to the light. I never heard him, like he was ignoring me, which only added to my anger!

What did I know about all this, virtually nothing, and yet Ginger was right. "Why hadn't my dad ever talked to me? I never felt him or heard him! She had to be right, didn't she?

Asking for Guidance

I prayed for answers and a few weeks later on a warm sunny morning while watering my garden, and asking God "Please Father I need some advice, I don't know what to do. Please help me help your child, my son. I need some help down here."

Out of nowhere, I began to chant. I didn't know where these words were coming from, as I had never done this before. Everything inside of me felt this was God answering me, as the words began to flow out of my mouth.

tongue)

"I call upon the Great Divine to banish this entity from this son of mine," I said it out loud. I put the hose down ran inside and grabbed a pen and paper and wrote the words that were coming through me.

"I call upon the Great Divine to banish this entity from this son of mine! I demand in the name of Creator that you go to the light and let my son Adam be free! Banish the attachment thru time and space and to the light shall it be embraced. Entity Go NOW – Flee! Release my son Adam Let him be! Through the light, you will soar returning to this bloodline no more!"

Once I finished writing, I heard, "Then it will end."

I looked at the clock it was 10:20 there was an urgency running through me. I didn't have much time. I called Ginger and Danielle and told them what had happened. I had to have two other people to chant with me starting at 11:00 AM. We had to repeat the incantation three times. They both agreed to help me.

At 11:00 AM Danielle was on the phone with me. I called in Archangel Michael for protection as Danielle, and I began the incantation. Ginger was at home playing her drum while repeating the chant. Every fiber in me knew I was fighting for my son's life!

As we began, I felt the heaviest feeling, a tightness I had never known in my chest. I can only describe it as something holding on and refusing to let go. On the second uttering of the words, it got even tighter, almost as if it was fighting back to stop me. It wasn't until the third time, with tears streaming down my face something broke free. I felt it release! The pressure was gone.

I now cried tears of joy. Everything in me knew whatever it was we had just unattached it from Adam and sent it into the room of transformation.

Danielle was also sobbing as she explained the pressure in her chest, and then felt the moment of release!

Immediately my phone rang. Caller ID showed it was Ginger. I hung up with Danielle and clicked over. "What in the world was that?" I exclaimed!

She laughed, "It wasn't in this world. I felt the pressure in my chest and the release."

We talked for a few minutes; my mind was twirling, I couldn't rationalize what I had just experienced.

It had to be said at 11:00 because by the time we got to the third chant, it was 11:11. That is when the gateway to heaven is open. Three people had to perform the incantation as three, represents the Holy Trinity.

As I sat outside later that afternoon talking to mom about all of this, I felt her, and I knew she was there. Aloud I wanted her to answer, but she was silent. I felt a male presence; it wasn't Bubba. I didn't know who it was, as he stood behind my Mom. I had reached a heightened state whereby through my third eye I could perceive and see things. I saw my dad, and he was smiling. He whispered to me, "Thank you."

But this was freaky, what was happening? Had he been the attachment I wondered. Why was he thanking me?

That was all he said, and then my parents were both were gone.

I was in a state of confusion as I sat there wondering what this was all about.

That night I dreamed of an old friend I hadn't talked to in a while. When I woke up, I thought *why was he in my dream?*

I had worked with Doug in Houston. He had such a passionate heart and a personality bigger than life! He was knowledgeable on many topics. He grew up in an area where as he put it, voodoo and magic were the norms. Through the years he had become a brother and had shared many tails of his experiences. I thought perhaps I was being guided to him for answers I picked up the phone and entered his number.

After our hello's and family inquiries, I said "Doug, I had something happen that I am trying to understand, and you came to my mind. That's why I am calling I want your input."

"Okay, I'll give it a shot sister, what happened?"

I began to tell him and then I asked, "So do you have any idea what happened? Was it my dad attached to Adam?"

He was silent for a while before he answered, "I don't think so, from what you just told me I think your Dad was trying to protect your son."

"What?" I questioned. "I don't understand."

He laughed and proclaimed, "Girl, from what you are telling me, you broke what is called a Hundred Year Curse put on the men in your family!"

To say I was in shock was an understatement! I had to think about this.

I loved my dad and I was daddy's little girl, however, my dad and I had a complicated relationship. He was an alcoholic, which led to a lot of disappointments and heartaches. Bubba who was my dad's first born son had been in prison. I lost my first son Brandon. Danielle had miscarried a twin son her first pregnancy and carried Dante to term, a surprising outcome. Adam had been dealing with depression, alcohol, and drugs. It all made sense in my heart and mind. In my being, I knew it was true. Perhaps I came in this lifetime with the intention to heal the males in my father's bloodline.

After all I had come to understand that I had experienced some pretty unexplainable things so far in my life! Who was I to question it!

I have since felt that my dad stayed to help Bubba, and once Bubba reconnected with Christ Consciousness, perhaps he then stayed to help Adam, his bloodline, and his first living biological grandson.

As one of my teachers taught me, "People, you just can't make this stuff up!"

The more I studied attachments; I felt drawn to want to help others that were having the same experiences.

I found a course on the web "Spiritual Releases and Healing," as taught by John Livingston. In my excitement and desire to understand, I discussed it with Ginger. Through this information, I discovered his particular teaching was working with God, Jesus and Archangel's. I knew of Michael, and now I was being introduced to Raphael and Gabriel. I also discovered you cannot do this without permission from the client, every soul has free will and permission must be given.

That made sense, I had asked Adam for his permission. I then spoke with Danielle and Anne who had no reservations. Mark, however, was a different story. I don't think he entirely understood what I was doing, all he heard was dark forces, and entities and that resulted in fear for my well being. I told him I was working with light beings. I was secure in that protection. I saw the look of concern in his eyes; therefore, I did a cord cutting, releasing me of his fear.

I knew this was part of my journey. I do not recommend that everyone can or should do this. There are case studies of many that have done Spirit Release and Healing; who took on their client's illness.

As a determined mother, I was going to save my child. I asked and trusted God found the way, why question it!

It was also that same summer at a neighborhood barbecue that I discovered one of my neighbor's beliefs. Emily was a retired school teacher. She was a tall studious sixty-six-year-old blonde. We were discussing books and found we had recently read the same book in which one of the characters was a flamboyant psychic. I led the conversation to my beliefs. I did not know she had similar views until she quietly asked, "Have you ever had a psychic reading?"

I replied, "No, I went to a gypsy at a festival and had a palm reading in my twenties. Fifteen years later I went back to the festival, and to my surprise, she was the same palm reader. When she took my hand, she said 'I've read your palm before.' That was wild!"

Emily said, "Really." She then leaned over closer to me and whispered, "I have a friend in Houston named Patricia who's a psychic. She owns a shop and does readings there. I can call you with her info if you're interested."

A psychic, yes that sounded exciting; this was something I had never done before!

I called Ginger that afternoon, and we agreed on a road trip!

I contacted the shop a few times and could not get a hold of Patricia. The last time I called I told the clerk why I was calling. He explained Patricia was out on a family emergency. He then referred me to a friend named Alex that was a fabulous reader.

She was booked two weeks out. I made appointments for Ginger and me for the next available dates.

I was in ah of all the information that Alex gave me and most of the time I laughed when she was talking. Because before she could tell me what spirit said to her, I heard the answers.

She asked, "You're hearing them, aren't you?"

I shrugged and answered, "Yes, but I don't understand them all of the time. I get a few words and figure out what they're trying to say."

She said, "Honey you hear them and the more you use your psychic abilities, the stronger they will get, it's just another muscle."

I never thought of it that way, and I now share that with others in the Connecting with the Spiritual Realm workshops that I teach.

Some of the things that came through were Bubba's jokes and personality. Wow, how did she know that? Mom told her how much she loved the gingersnap cookies I baked last week.

Which brought a smile to my face and heart, she still loved her sweets. There were many confirmations that she heard my loved ones.

Then out of nowhere, she asked, "Are you a witch? I'm hearing you are doing some powerful stuff!"

"I don't know what I am." I answered then I asked, "Did I help my dad go to the light?"

She listened then replied with an awestruck look on her face. "I am hearing you broke a Century Curse."

I shook my head "yes," and then answered in search for more explanation, "That's what I was told. I still can't understand it, and if dad's in the light why can't I hear him?" I asked.

She closed her eyes and appeared to be listening and then answered, "He is now in the light. I hear 'he is asleep.'"

Then she explained her belief that when a soul first crosses over they are not in consciousness, the soul is what some call a classroom to understand what lesson's they learned during that lifetime.

Then she looked at me and asked, "Are you writing a book?"

I laughed and answered, "My friend and I have joked about writing a book about two magical sisters."

She asked again. "No, are you writing a book?"

I answered, "I thought I was going to write a book a few years back. I have a title and the first two thousand words, but nothing came of it."

She said, "I don't know which book but I keep hearing '*the book*,' so I think you need to get busy on the book."

Never giving it a second thought that they weren't speaking of the story Ginger and I had recently talked about writing. So many things occurred during the next five months. Ginger and I discussed and wrote our outline for the book. I was hearing but not clearly, I continued to study Spirituality and performed Release and Healing of Spiritual Attachments.

Late That Summer

One afternoon I received a message that I couldn't get out of my mind, "There aren't enough souls on the other side to fight the battle."

I repeated to Danielle what I heard. After helping me with the release, we often spoke on the topic, and I continued to help her understand, the best way that I could.

A week later Danielle called to tell me, "You aren't going to believe this! At church today the preacher said, 'We're engaged in a Spiritual war, and there aren't enough souls on the other side to fight the battle!"

Chills ran down me. I answered, "It sounds like all who are listening are getting the same message."

If Danielle had any reservations about "Connecting with Spirit" they were now put to rest.

As for me after receiving the confirmation that many are hearing the same call, I continued to study and practice Spirit Release, and proclaiming, "I am a Lightworker, a Warrior of Archangel Michael!"

Ginger and I had become even closer, we became sisters. We were performing releases together with the guidance and protection of God, Jesus, Archangel Michael, Archangel Gabriel, Archangel Raphael, and the mighty Warriors of Light on Earth, It felt so right to be helping others. This part of our individual journey was to work together, helping other souls cross to the light. By the fall of 2012 through referrals we were getting request from others, we cleared homes, offices, hotels. We removed attachments from people. One of our psychic friends called and asked us to clear an old 1800 building in Galveston that she was going to be doing an event at, she wanted to make certain there was nothing there that could attach to her. I heard cries of joy when they were sent to the light that rainy evening.

When we began this work, I would see faces through my mind's eye that were somewhat demonic looking; it was as if they were watching me. The information I had studied did not mention that this could happen, nor was it happening to Ginger.

I somehow knew to call upon Archangel Michael to escort the entities away from me, and once I called him, they would disappear. I was not afraid to do the work as I felt this was what I was being called to do. Again, I remind you I do not recommend that anyone just jump into Spiritual Clearings out of curiosity or for excitement. If you are guided by Spirit to do this work, you will know. As much as we may not want to believe it, there is light and dark in everything and darkness feeds off the energy of light and attaches to a speck of fear.

Choose Your Words Wisely

Also, I need to mention a valuable lesson I learned that fall of 2012.

Every night before I go to bed, I light candles saying my prayers and giving gratitude. It was with a joyful heart; I was lighting the candles I said "Thank you God and thank you to all the Spiritual light beings. I love you all as I invite Spirit into my life."

Strange or extraordinary things began to happen in my home over the next week. I would find cabinet doors open, and items moved around, I would hear whistling in the other room. Lights were on that I knew I hadn't turned on. I was the only one in the house. Cici, my beautiful Jack Russell Terrier companion, would growl and bark like crazy as if there was something there. I would walk through the house yelling, "Hello" only to receive no answer. One night the printer in the other room woke me up printing blank pages!

At first I thought it was Bubba; usually, when something like this or out of the ordinary would occur I would say, "Bubba behave," and I would hear a chuckle. However, I never heard him. He never answered me, but Bubba liked to play jokes on me, so I assumed it was him.

That following weekend there was a full moon. Ginger came over and spent the night as we had planned a ceremony. The next morning, we were sitting out in the garden while drinking a cup of coffee she said, "I know this may sound strange, but I swear someone crawled in bed with me last night."

I laughed and said, "Probably Bubba, he's been here all week pulling pranks."

We shrugged it off after all she and I had seen and done some astonishing things together.

Alex and I had become friends and checked in with each other. We discovered we had the same last maiden name, as well as a Spiritual connection. Late that afternoon while talking with Alex, I told her Ginger thought someone crawled into bed with her. We laughed about it and then I said, "Is there someone other than my relatives in my house?"

We sat in silence for what seemed like a full minute then she said, "I heard 'yes.' and you invited him in, although he's not malevolent."

I was stunned, "I invited him?"

"He looks like a dandy, a gentleman from the 1920 or 30's. He's got the handle bar mustache. I see a vest with a pocket watch. He's in awe of the technology. He's looking for a little girl, and he doesn't wish to harm you."

I said, "I didn't invite him!"

She asked, "When did you start noticing him?"

"It's been about a week."

By now she knew me pretty well. "Okay sister, so what ceremony did you do before you noticed someone there?" She asked.

I had to think back when I heard "Candles."

I said, "The only thing I can think of is the candle ceremony that I do every night."

"What do you say or do when you light them?" She asked.

"Well, I say the light of God prayer and I thank God and the Spiritual Realm, and then I invite them in to help me my life."

She laughed and said, "Okay so you asked him." Then explained, "Imagine you are hanging out up there and you hear 'I invite Spirit in, and then suddenly you see a portal open. You jump through it for a visit, that's kind of how it works. One thing I can say is Honey you were lucky because that portal could have allowed more than one to come through. He was just in the right place at the right time."

I thought about it for a moment and then asked, "Okay so how do I get rid of him?"

"You politely ask him to leave, tell him this is your home, you wish him no harm, but he needs to return to the light. Request that the angels escort him out of your home."

I took her advice and did exactly that!

That evening when I told Ginger about it, then said, "It was probably him that crawled into bed with you! I must not have been his type since he was here for a week and never got in bed with me." We had a good laugh.

I am grateful that I learned a valuable lesson in the power of our words that night. Thank goodness, I had adopted the Unity Prayer in my ceremony and repeated it as I lit the candles. "The Light of God Protects Me, The Light of God surrounds Me, The Light of God is in Me, Where I am God Is," each time I light my white candle.

My intention was to invite Spiritual Light Beings, Archangel's, Guides, Ascended Masters. Perhaps the spiritual light beings knew I needed a little lesson, for there is no telling what I could have let in that night.

I adopted a new nightly spiritual practice after that. I light candles in prayer and Grateful Gratitude; one for the white light of God, another for Archangel's and Ascended Masters,

149

one for my Angels and Guides, and sometimes another for a particular person. However, I now choose my words very carefully.

CHAPTER 12

Road Trip - Galveston Here We Come

It was now summer of 2013 time for a to visit Galveston Texas. I grew up an hour from Galveston and spent a lot of time there in my youth, but I hadn't been there in years. However, it seemed the perfect setting for the story Ginger, and I had decided to write. Knowing the area gave it authenticity. Now we were on our way to do some research and get a geographical feel of the island for the book.

We had planned the trip so that we would be there for Full Moon. To be on the beach under her fullness sounded heavenly.

The first three days there would be work, and then we'd take a break on the full moon. After gathering information from the locals, we drove around until we were familiar with the island. We noted street names, selected houses, and restaurants that would be in the story. We had a GPS but it was more fun to drive and dictate the directions, scenery, and surroundings into a recorder. We got to know the island and wanted to highlight the flavor and uniqueness of Galveston.

In our travels, we discovered a metaphysical shop on the island. We planned to visit it and purchase a Ouija Board, with the idea of the full moon being the perfect time to contact the Spiritual Realm of our loved ones.

Until then I had never stepped inside a metaphysical shop. I had been to the local rock shop to buy crystals. I bought Oracle cards in a bookstore or on the computer. I was very excited to discover, "The Witchery" and all it held within its doors.

We strolled into the shop one afternoon. I would compare myself to a kid in a candy store as I looked around at all the stones, cards, statues, jewelry, and books. While scanning the bookshelves, a book fell off the shelf. I glanced at the front cover and put it back on the shelf. I moved down the shelf, and the book flipped face up in front of me onto the floor as if someone threw it.

I looked around to find no one there, then picked it up and placed it back on the shelf. As I read the title, Thirty Day Dream Journey with the Archangel's. I thought *hmm this sounds interesting. But not exactly what I had in mind.* I continued to stroll to the next section when I heard the book hit the floor again.

I thought *okay I've read and heard others speak about books falling off shelves in front of them. That was three times.* Something or someone was trying to get my attention. *I'm supposed to read this book.*

I bought the book along with a few others, one on Angel Magic, and another on Angel Numbers. I had started noticing I saw the same times on the clock, like **11:11, 2.22, 4.44 5.55.** I was eager to understand their meaning.

That night Ginger and I had dinner, and then at dusk, we went down to the beach and sat under the full moon; there was an intense energy in the air. When we returned to the hotel, we lit white candles and pulled out the Ouija Board. We each got a pen and paper. Now we would ask the question and write the letters as our fingers guide us. Next, we would translate the words that would appear transcendentally.

We began with a prayer as we atoned the corners of the board with Holy Water and called on Archangel Michael for protection, with my previous experience with Spirit and portals this was a must.

Ginger said, "You Go First."

I talked to my mom and Bubba. In honesty, it had been a while since I had heard from them. I was still trying to understand so many things, confusion was a giant part of my journey in searching for my truth. I asked questions that only they would know the answers to, receiving verification that I was talking to them. I received loving messages from them and my dad that night as I wrote down the letters and put them together in a completed word or sentence. For me this was again a confirmation I needed that they were still with me.

Once I finished, I asked Ginger, "Who do you want to talk to?"

Ginger had a sweet conversation with her mom and sister.

I asked, "Is there any other loved ones for Ginger or me that would like to give a message?"

When my hand started moving, Ginger wrote down the letters.

We began figuring out the message that read Charlie for Ginger.

Bewildered she said, "I don't know anyone by the name of Charlie that has passed over."

We decided to take a break so that she could ponder who this might be. As we sat out on the balcony in the moon light, Ginger appeared to be in deep thought. It was over a half an hour later when she looked at me and said, "Peter's father's name is Charles, but I didn't know that he had transcended. Peter hasn't spoken to him in years. But you would think that if he had passed someone would have called. If Peter knew he would have told me."

She was in disbelief as we said our prayer and called on Archangel Michael. Then Ginger asked, "Charles Madison is that you?"

Our fingers were guided to the word, "YES!"

She was astonished when she began to ask him questions and made the confirmation that it was indeed her ex-husband. She was given information on his death, and a beautiful, loving message of regrets and asking forgiveness.

After we had returned home, Ginger called her son Peter and told him what had happened. He was in utter shock, and reported to her he didn't have any inkling about his dad. He hadn't heard that he had died, but then again he hadn't spoken to him in a couple of years. But he was going to check into it."

After over a week of investigating, Peter confirmed his dad had died six months before our full moon experience with him.

I was dumbfounded at the event. I learned a few more things that night; all souls want our forgiveness for any heartache they caused us when they were here. But also, that when someone on the other side has a message, and you are open to receive that message, it will come.

CHAPTER 13
Dreaming with the Archangels

After returning from our Galveston trip, a few weeks passed before I picked up the book *Thirty Day Dream Journey with the Archangels*. However, once I began reading it and realized it was a thirty-day guide to bring the spiritual realm alive in your dream world. I was intrigued.

Each night an Archangel would travel with you in your dreams. Putting your free will in motion, you first do an exercise and an affirmation to open your energy up to that Archangel and where you will travel to in your dream world. Next, you are instructed to write down who and what are in your dreams; people, places, scenery, animals, etc. They call these human characters and non-human characters. Through the process, you begin to create your personal dream symbol cards. As you work through the process, you begin to understand the meaning of the symbol when it appears in your dream. An example would be a snake. Over time I began to recognize that the snake was calling my attention to something that needed healing in my life. However, unbeknown to me it also was awakening me to study healing modalities in the future.

Next, anytime you wake up during the night you are instructed to write down what you remember of the dream for recall the next morning. It could be a name, a person, an animal or an object, or you could have heard a message. The key was to write down anything from your dream, when you're half asleep. The next morning working with the Archangel Uriel there is an affirmation for recall, and you begin to untangle the messages that came in the dream. Once you have all the information from your dream, you then relate it back to what is going on in your life. Ultimately to receive the message Spirit or loved ones on the other side are sending you.

It is explained that through the thirty day period, you work with four Archangel's; Archangel Michael, Archangel Gabriel, Archangel Raphael, and Archangel Uriel. I was excited! I would now be working with yet another Archangel by the name of Uriel.

I had never tried anything like this before. Although I had heard of those that kept dream journals to help them translate their dreams, I had never tried it. *This was going to be an adventure!* I thought. With a life of prophetic dreaming, this was to me the icing on the cake!

Day 1 –I was enthusiastic to get started. That evening I lit my candles in gratitude to Creator and one for Archangel Michael's protection. I read the ceremony affirmations then turned out the light. When I awoke in the night, I wrote down what I heard, saw or felt in my dreams. The next morning I followed the program and performed the exercise with Archangel Uriel. I did recall my dream as I sat and cried and talked to God. I understood the message I received that night was to help me heal even deeper from all the losses in my life. The message was one of love and brought about in me a knowing that I am taken care of, and no matter what, I am not alone.

Day 2 – Day 4 – I didn't recall anything, nothing, not a thing! I slept so soundly that I didn't remember waking up to write anything down. I know we always dream, but I didn't remember anything. Every morning I tried, and every morning I would hear one word, "Patience."

My ego was running ramped, "What made you think you could do this? You must be doing something wrong," that little voice in my head that wants to be in control and doesn't like change. It reminds me of Pac-man, as it slowly chomps away at anything in its path to win the game.

Through years of studying and fighting with my ego; I discovered the ego is frightened by change and doesn't want you to "**Remember Who You Are**." Archangel Michael reminds us that you can do anything because **You are a child of God.**

I got up my will power as I thought; *"So are you going to let your ego win and just stop trying?"* Followed by, *"Not on your life; I think I'll just start over with Day 1 and work this."* I was meant to do this or that book would not have dropped in front of me! I can do it!

That night I returned to **Day 1**, and I put all my focus and intention (*key word intention*) into it. I wanted something fascinating to happen and to understand the messages given or spoken to me. I told myself; *"I did this once I could do this again!"*

Day 1 – This time I put a paper and pen near me in the bed, (which the authors suggest). When I awoke through the night, I wrote down things I remembered. The next morning I read what I wrote, which made no sense. I followed the program and asked Archangel Uriel to help me recall the dream. I went downstairs and got my coffee and walked out on the back deck. I love sitting out in nature in the morning watching the world come to life. Taking it all in as I am bringing on the day, in the morning calm I feel his presence as I talk to God. After my morning prayer, I started a conversation with Archangel Uriel about my dream.

Immediately like a projector playing, I saw my dream like a movie as it came to life in my mind. There were stairs, I was running late. I ran up the stairs and tripped.

The next scene was a slow-moving stream. I thought about it for a moment then said aloud, "I still don't understand what that means?" Then it was as if a light bulb lit up in my mind and I knew the answer "Divine Timing!" I pulled an oracle card for further understanding, Spirit never ceases to amaze me, the card I drew was *Divine Timing*, which read, you are reaching new heights of spiritual understand as this occurs stay in the flow. There is no time but Creator's to arrive. You can disappoint your ego, but you can never disappoint God. I then understood the metaphor of the stairs and the stream.

Day 2 – I awoke, I was talking to someone. The only thing I remembered was being elated with joy. I had to go to the restroom and then I heard Archangel Uriel telling me, "Remember to write down your dreams." I got out of bed, and by the time I got back to bed to write keywords that would trigger my recall, they were gone. You know how sometimes you are dreaming and you wake up to go to the restroom and by the time you get there, you can't remember the dream. The only word I wrote during the night was, "Happy!" I tried the recall exercise the next morning, but with nothing to trigger my memory, I thought, here we go again!

Day 3 – I awoke and wrote down a few words, God's Love, a Mom's Love. The recall was a little more difficult and without a lot of information. As the day went on, I continued to talk to Archangel Uriel and felt I understood the message as God's Love is a Mother's Love, unconditional. The Father-Mother God, the Creator. We are all his children. We are loved.

Day 4 – I dreamed of a Book called "God's Love," and a bright blinding light at the end of a hall. I wasn't in the dream but was watching the dream. I was experiencing a lucid dream. I hadn't done this before as I traveled and met my Spirit Guide.

Suddenly I snapped out of the dream and wrote.

"I don't know how I knew, but I knew I was in the Heavenly Realm and the light was the Light of God. I asked my guide, 'What is God's Love?'"

I heard a soft voice reply, "Unconditional."

The next morning no recall was needed as I understood the message I had received the night before was given again to help me further understand the dream of day 3, or was perhaps a confirmation given to me to reinforce that I did understand.

After this night things began to come alive in my dream world.

One of my favorite dreams I awoke one morning and leaped off the bed with my arms stretched in front of me and in my excitement, I exclaimed loudly, "This is so much fun!" I was soaring with the Angels through the clouds.

Their energy was extraordinarily beautiful with many indescribable colors more brilliant than anything I had ever seen. We laughed as they were teaching me to fly, or was I remembering as I soared with them? I could see the universe! It was stunning!

Another morning as I awoke to hear the words, "Pure White Light," as if someone whispered in my ear. I drifted back into my dream world, this time I was met by a presence engulfed with a glowing white light. Who was this?

The presence had a very masculine yet lovingly soft tone, "You are in the light. Feel the light as it surrounds you." I felt warm and safe. My heart exploded with happiness and was full of joy. Next, I was soaring through the universe.

I wasn't sure if I had traveled to a higher Spiritual Realm it was more as if I had merged with air. There was no weight of the physical body. Out of nowhere a mist of glowing blue light surrounded me and ignited a flame within me. I was now the illuminating white light, spinning higher and higher in the light, yet I was the light. I knew I was safe, protected and loved. I had just met Archangel Michael.

On many occasions, I was talking with someone in my dream world, and when I awoke, I felt I had been in a classroom. I would go to the restroom and forget by the time I got back to bed. Somehow, I knew this was okay; I trusted that the messages were always there for me and I began to call them "downloads for later."

Once I awoke refreshed and I knew I had been talking with the Holy Archangel Gabriel.

I was committed to my journey and learned more about who I am, and the connection with Spirit. The connection we all have. "Thank you, Father-Mother God."

To get a deeper meaning, I had the thought to write down the times that I awoke. I wanted to understand how they coincided with the dreams. I used the book I had purchased by Doreen Virtue on Angel Numbers. I summarized that part of the meaning of my dream was in the explanation of the times on the clock. I then added the Angel Dream Oracle cards to my morning practice. I took the extra steps, and the process became very in depth. However, it was worth it! My passion for understanding was driving me on.

I realized all the astral journeys were essential, but the ones I remembered were most important as they were healing dreams. One, in particular, I walked into an auditorium, I looked around the room which was full of women. I saw my mom and my maternal grandmother waiting for me. With one on each side of me, we walked up a long aisle, passing all theses graceful, smiling women. In a whisper, I asked my mom, "Who are they?"

She whispered, "They heard you were coming and these are all of your female ancestors who desired to greet you."

I felt a most magnificent feeling of **Belonging and Support.**

Something even more astounding than I ever believed possible happened. I walked with Jesus during one of my dreams. I saw us walking hand in hand and talking.

Then we approached this most extraordinary blinding white light of God energy, and I began to cry. My heart was overflowing with the love I felt. I found I couldn't look directly at the light, but I didn't have to, it engulfed me.

My entry read. I walked with Jesus last night, how beautiful he is. He led me down the beach, and I met the Father. I awoke with tears streaming down my face, tears of overwhelming love. I knew with my every fiber deep within my soul I sat at the foot of God and I was euphoric!

Through the dreams, I met my Spirit Guide, Guardian Angel, Archangels, God, Jesus and I visited my deceased loved ones. When I say, I met them, it was a knowing in my soul, the energy of the light being. I didn't always remember the dreams but I had the knowing of the being I met.

With my loved ones, sometimes I saw them and sometimes I recognized their soul energy.

With the Archangels and Angels, I saw beautiful colors of glowing light. I heard the angel's choir around me. I awoke every morning so joyful and so at peace.

I am so grateful that the Archangels persistently dropped that book in front of me, knowing exactly how to reach me.

Will everyone have the same experiences? No. We're all unique and given the information we are in need of at the time on our journey.

For me, I felt it was to combat my ego. To reinforce my belief that the Spiritual Realm is real and alive within all of us, as well as to help me heal my heart. These dreams were happening I wasn't making it up!

Once I finished the thirty-day exercises in my excitement I had the thought *there were four Archangels in that book; there have to be more!*

Once again, I was on a quest to further my Spiritual Growth.

PART III
Impeccable
Trust and Faith

CHAPTER 14
Discovering and Exploring

After the dream journey, I was so excited I spent the next several months dedicated to studying the Angels. Part three, Impeccable Trust and Faith; I learned that sometimes you just have to surrender to find what you are searching for.

I had such a burning desire to understand and in my search for more information I found books on the Angels by Billy Graham, Robert Grant, and Doreen Virtue to name a few. I also discovered Doreen Virtue taught workshops on the subject. I ordered a deck of "Archangel Oracle" cards. I could hardly contain my excitement when they arrived. I immediately opened them and began to read the instruction booklet.

I was surprised to find that they each have specialties, aura colors and crystals associated with them. Up until this point I had worked with four, I wasn't aware there were thousands!

I asked questions and I began to hear them in my mind. Of course, once again my ego was entering and serving up doubt.

In the fall of 2013 I was in a conversation with Alex I told her, "I am hearing other voices, not just my relatives, yet sometimes, it sounds like my voice answering me."

She got quiet as she was listening to Spirit for answers.

She gave a short giggle, and replied, "You are connecting with the Angels."

I answered in excitement, "I knew it!" Then asked, "Am I talking with Archangel Michael or which one?"

She quickly answered, "I'm hearing Yes and many others."

Why I needed confirmation that I was talking with them, I don't know, call me human. I believed it, but part of me expected this large Spiritual Light Being with Wings to stand in front of me and talk to me. I wasn't aware how rare that was and not everyone would have that kind of experience.

I was communicating with angels, and I knew very little about them. I had attended many churches over the years searching for more than someone else's interpretation of Spirit. I had never found it, no one ever talked about Angels other than what was written in the holy books.

Not long after the conversation with Alex, through my studies I discovered that one of the ways the Spiritual realm speaks to me was called claircogniance; meaning "clear knowing." Hence it would sound like my own voice when I heard the answers. I became more and more comfortable calling on the Archangel's and began to ask them for help with everyday life. I was testing the waters so to speak, the doubting Thomas. If I lost an item I would call on Archangel Chamuel (the finding angel) to help me find it, and it never failed, I would hear (in my mind) where to look, or I would see where it was in my mind. I always found what I was looking for. In busy parking lots I would call on Archangel Raphael (who helps us with travel) and his parking angels to find me a parking spot. A parking spot always became available when I needed it. If I was running late I would ask Archangel Metatron to bind time, I arrived on time with no problems. Some would call this a coincindence; I believed that there was something deeper going on.

I also found Spiritual exercises to help me build my confidence in what I was hearing, seeing, knowing, and feeling. I practiced them with Ginger and my daughters when they visited. I felt like a child again. This was exciting; picture a child on Christmas Eve; the impatience building up to Christmas morning, the anticipation and the thrill of opening their gifts. That's exactly how I felt when I would see or hear the answers.

During one particular exercise Ginger and I tried seeing who in the Spirit world was around us. This type of communication is called; Psychometry.

I sat with my eyes closed and held Ginger's ring in my hand. I began to see a man standing behind her. As I described what he looked like she immediately knew this to be her maternal grandfather. Next, I saw a small girl in a closet playing with a doll. Ginger confirmed when she was a small girl she made a playhouse in her closet to hide from her family. I will not go into detail, as the message for her was a very personal and emotional one of healing.

We took a short break then Ginger sat down and closed her eyes. She held a piece of my jewelry in one hand, holding my hand in the other. She began to say, "There is a Native American woman standing behind you. She has dark hair, and wears a white dress, she is beautiful. I get the feeling she's an Indian Princess." Then Ginger said, "Wow, a white wolf walked up and is standing beside her." The maiden said, "'tell her we have been with her since she was a child. Tell her I am called; she who walks with wolves. I am one of her guides.'"

I was in shock as the long-forgotten memory of the white wolf flooded my mind and came to life in my third eye. I whispered, "It was real."

Ginger looked at me in confusion. Then I relayed my childhood experience of meeting the white wolf. We sat and talked about it. We both agreed, now that I had become aware of the spiritual realm; this was spirits way of confirming to me, that this did happen, and that Spirit had been working to reach me for many years.

What is my life purpose, my mission?

After I took the dream journey with the Archangel's my dream world was alive and very vivid. I began to question what is my life purpose, what path am I to take? What am I to do with all I've learned?

I asked so often I'd turn blue and then in a dream an angel came.

In my dream, I was standing at a fork in the road literally, when a beautiful Angel appeared beside me.

I asked, "Which road do I take?"

She softly spoke and gestured with a sweep of her wing, "This one or this one," as she pointed to each path "One leads to the other and both will get you to your destination. One will be smooth, the other rocky. The choice is yours."

I woke up and said aloud to the walls, "well, that didn't tell me anything."

Her answer was one I have thought about many times, as it describes mankind choices. I have heard and read "be in service". In talking with Archangel Michael, I understood it to mean service could be as simple as helping a friend move, calling to check on a friend, smiling at strangers, giving kind words. Being in service doesn't mean choosing a spiritual profession. Being in service is having compassion in helping others. It's not doing something for someone because you feel you can't say "No," it's doing something for someone because in your heart you truly want to help them. As long as we are being in service with love in our heart, well that in itself is the mission.

For several months now, at least once a week, during my morning Spiritual practice I drew the "Energy Healing" card, I didn't know much about energy healing, but the card said "You are a healer, pick a modality."

I procrastinated but finally overcame my ego. I decided to sign up for a class in Healing Touch. I was finally going to learn how energy healing works.

As the time approached for the class I was excited. Then an unusual thing happened, the day before the class I got two phone calls. One from the business organizing the class confirming my registration, the other later in the day from the instructor who told me the class was being moved to her home. But I would need to find another person to attend because I would need a partner. If I couldn't find a partner the class would be canceled.

171

That was bizarre! I was totally confused.

I was really disappointed that I wouldn't be taking the class. I still had so many questions on energy healing. There must have been some reason this instructor was not going to teach me.

That night I read an article on how to see your own aura. How intriguing, I performed the exercise and my aura was green. I immediately thought I was sick. I searched the internet for meanings of aura colors only to find a green aura meant *healer*.

I was relieved, but then my question to Spirit was, "How do I know what to do? Please show me, tell me, I need some answers down here."

Yes, I enjoy talking with Spirit like an old friend.

That night I had the most vivid dream of colors. I was standing looking at a tunnel spinning like a funnel full of colors. As I stood and admired it an Angel appeared. I recognized her as the same Angel that was at the fork in the road dream.

She again gestured with one wing sweeping it toward the tunnel and gently said, "Walk through the colors' for healing."

Softly she took my hand and led me into the tunnel.

The next morning, I knew I now had a new mission to understand healing with color! This is called chromo-therapy. I discovered colored walls were used in the hospitals until the 1950's when they began to paint them white. *Was there something to using color with healing? Why was I shown this?*

There were so many things to study, one lead to another, so much information to digest. I decided to put energy healing on the back burner for now. I found it very easy to become confused by the views of others. I wanted to understand more about the Archangel's and I truly wanted to take a workshop from Doreen Virtue, but she didn't offer them in Texas; therefore, I plowed on. I asked questions to Archangel Michael, I kept asking. I listened and follow what I heard. I discovered that is exactly what we are supposed to do.

I was now working with the Archangels constantly; I asked them for help daily. I had now asked Archangel Michael to give me courage and lead me toward my life mission. To fill me with confidence and to help me surrender anything that was blocking my path. I had asked Archangel Uriel to light my path and show me the way and Archangel Chamuel to help me find what I was looking for, because honestly, I didn't have a clue.

Overtime I began to know the angels' different energies when I felt them around me. I laughed and joked with them, I developed a friendship with them. I was excited to discover and watch as God's plan for me unfolded. However as with anything in life there would be speed bumps along the way and for me lots of deep healing. Thank you, Father-Mother God for your beautiful messengers.

A Conversation with Jesus

Through organized religion at an early age I had accepted Jesus into my heart; I will never forget the feeling. However, I never prayed to him, I always prayed to God. I knew his teachings of love, and I knew the story the Bible gave us of Jesus. I believed he died for his love of mankind. I knew he loved me. However, I never truly got to know him, within myself I began to ask questions and search for the answers.

In a meditation, I was sitting on a rock by a stream when out of nowhere the most peaceful presence touched my right shoulder. I looked up into the most loving amber eyes that I recognized as Jesus. I stood up to greet him like an old friend. We strolled beside the stream as I explained my confusion and concerns. Before we parted the last thing, he said was, "Your walk will require impeccable trust and faith."

After this meditation, I thought about our conversation and realized for me I would still call Jesus, Brother, Friend and Teacher.

Not long after that I had been reading about automatic writing, a practice something like an interview. You write down your questions, or ask them aloud, then write down everything that comes to your mind. With some people their handwriting changes as Spirit takes over providing answers to the questions.

I decided to try my hand at it. I called upon Archangel Michael for protection, and began asking questions. I asked to speak to my dad, which I did! We had a wonderful loving emotional conversation. He also said I'd begin having visions, he now understood I had been having them all of my life, and apologized for not understanding. That same year after our encounter, the visions became stronger, on numerous occasions I saw things before they happened.

After a beautiful conversation with my dad, Archangel Michael asked me, if there was anyone else I wanted to connect with?

Out of nowhere I heard myself say, "Jesus."

I wasn't surprised when I heard his sweet gentle voice reply softly, "I am right here my child and I know there are many questions you are seeking the answers for."

I began to cry, for reasons I didn't understand this was very emotional for me to hear his voice. After a brief moment, I asked, "What should I do next? What is my life purpose, what's my mission?

"There is a man coming to teach you, a good man, you will learn many things. Look for him."

"Then what am I to do?" I pleaded.

"Trust Me, Love Me, Teach of Me," he answered.

I sat there with tears rolling down my cheeks. I wasn't sure why, where, or how my path was going to unfold, but I was certain Spirit was guiding me.

CHAPTER 15
The Mystic

New Year's Eve brought with it a beautiful full moon. I had a ritual of burning candles on each full moon, this year I decided I would light them at midnight to bring in 2014, the year equated to a seven, which represents the Mystic. All numbers have a vibration, and a Spiritual meaning and the number seven is known as the number of the seeker, the lifelong searcher of truth. The number seven also represents the death of old beliefs and rebirth for all who were seeking their truth. The full moon is the most opportune time to let go of old thought processes and anything that no longer serves you. My intuition was telling me that this was going to be a year of deeper spiritual growth. I was all in!

At midnight while fireworks were lighting the sky, I lit candles and created my light show. I lit one white for the White Light of God, and one blue for the Archangel Michael's guidance and protection for 2014. Next, I lit three colored candles to Archangel Haniel (the goddess of the moon), one silver as I asked her to heighten my Spiritual gifts-one green asking her to facilitate physical healing and one magenta, asking her to evoke me in Divine Grace. I said my prayers as I drifted off to sleep. To my surprise when I got up the next morning the blue Archangel Michael candle was still burning. To me, this was a sign of Spirit at work. That candle burned for ten hours, the number ten represents New Beginnings, and I had no idea the New Year was going to be so exciting!

'The Balance: Awakening'

Over the last year and a half Ginger and I had finished our manuscript. We researched several options for publication. However, the publisher we chose wanted us to change several things in our work to fit in with their company beliefs, but we refused.

The gentleman that we were working with suggested we should self-publish and gave us a contact at one company in particular. We then went through the process of self-publishing. As we were doing our first edit, we both thought, who did we think we were? What made us believe that we could write a book? We took all the suggestions for rewrites that the publisher wanted us to do as a slap in the face! Of course, these thoughts were a sign of the ego stepping in.

However, that fall working very closely with Archangel Gabriel (the communication angel) and Archangel Uriel (the angel of bright ideas) during the birth of "The Balance: Awakenings." Now January 2014 it was online in e-book form and soft and hard copies.

I had passed a new business in our area several times, each time I would hear, "Stop here." I ignored the little voice until March of that year with books in hand I wandered into "This Rocks and Glitters." The plan was to ask them to stock "The Balance-Awakenings." That day I met the owner Margo, a tall brunette with bohemian style. When I looked around, I was so excited to see all these beautiful crystals. In my excitement, I began to explain which stones represented each of the Archangel's, and the specialty of that Archangel. I was teaching without realizing it. Margo and I talked in detail that afternoon about the Archangels and the story of The Balance. A friendship was born, and The Balance had a home.

On one of my visits to see Margo she told me that she had a customer recently that mentioned a teacher, a man who talked to the Angels. I didn't think much about it as I knew everyone could communicate with the Angel's and anyone in the Spiritual Realm if they are open to the idea and set the intention to connect, they will. Just as I knew everyone could hear their deceased loved ones if they were open and worked at it.

In April, my Spiritual Growth was going to take yet another leap.

A friend I knew from the nonprofit organization named Annette, owned a local fitness center, in search of additional outlets for The Balance.

One day in my travels I stopped and talked to her about stocking our book on consignment. During my conversation with Annette and Cindy a lady that worked there; Annette told me about a retreat that she and Cindy had gone to the prior weekend. It was a workshop on how we hear healing messages from the Spiritual world.

There would be another workshop next month and Annette invited me to go. I smiled but didn't answer. In her excitement to tell me more about the workshop Cindy began to tell me her experience on that day. "We were given an exercise to ask spirit a question and receive the answers." She said, "I didn't know what they wanted me to write. I went outside and sat there looked up and said, 'I don't know what I'm supposed to write.'"

Without thinking, I said, "So you wrote what you were hearing, and it turned out to be what you needed to hear not what the instructor wanted to hear."

She looked at me in surprise, "Yes, Wow, how did you know that?"

Without a thought, I answered, "It's what I just heard."

Annette turned around astonished and asked, "Dianne, do you hear Spirit?"

I shyly said, "Yes. I talk with the Archangels and my Deceased Loved Ones."

I was not prepared for the next question when she asked, "Do you give readings?"

I thought *I talk to God and my loved ones and the Archangel's and I get answers, I don't call that reading.* I hesitated then before I knew what happened I answered, "I do, for myself."

"Would you be interested in doing readings here? I'd love to offer a session with you once a week and we could book clients for you."

My ego was not by any means ready for it. I was nervous about doing it, but somehow, someway before I walked out of there I agreed to start the following month. Cindy said that would give her a few weeks to start booking clients.

I told her, "I don't want to be called a psychic. I'd prefer to be known as an Angel Mystic. Also, I don't know what to charge for them."

Cindy replied, "What about a basket for a love offering?"

I agreed that was a good idea.

When I got in my vehicle and drove away, I couldn't believe I just said yes to give Reading's publicly. I looked up, "Really God, you want me to do this? I don't know that I can do this."

As I drove home, I kept talking when I heard the answer as it came in a very loving yet stern voice, "It's time to help them awaken." My eyes filled with tears as they often did when I heard the voice of our Creator.

I said, "Me!" then asked, "You want me to do this? I don't know how to do this?"

"Oh beloved, I would not ask of you what you could not do. Do you not talk to me, and trust the answers you are given?"

I timidly replied, "Yes, but that's different, I understand the answers to my questions. I don't know that I can do that for other people."

Again, that inner voice of the ego said, "You can't do it, you don't know how. What if you give the wrong information?"

God knows your thoughts before you speak them, he gently nudged me, "There is No difference; provide them the answers you hear."

I took this as my mission as directed from above when God said to me, "It's time to help them awaken."

I felt part of my mission was to help others make the connection to the Spiritual Realm. Awaken to the Spiritual World and the awareness that we can communicate with them. I thought I'll explain the Archangel's as I do their readings.

Two weeks later I heard that Doreen Virtue was going to be giving a one-day interactive workshop in Austin. Excitingly I signed up and became a Certified Angel Card Reader.

Classes aren't necessary to hear, see, feel or know you are connected. They are to learn and practice your gifts to build confidence in yourself. No one that has booked an appointment with me has ever asked to see my certificates. These classes helped increase my knowledge, and in turn, lead me to Spiritual Teaching and helping others with their Spiritual Growth.

When the day came to read publicly, I was very nervous. I gathered sage, crystals, candles, and cards. Yes, my ego was actively attempting to dupe me. As I drove to Annette's, I invoked the presence of the Archangels and asked them to surround me. I talked with them the entire twenty-minute drive. Archangel Michael reminded me that I was in service and there was no need for concern or worry.

When I got there and set-up with my crystals, based on the advice I received recently in a dream, "Build a grid and Spirit will come."

I had faith that this would happen, I lit the sage and walked around cleansing and clearing the energies in the room, then, I lit a white candle, said a prayer and invited Spiritual Light beings to join me.

Cindy had set up two appointments for me. I asked Archangel Michael to bring loving healing messages for the two people. The first client came in, I said a prayer and within minutes I began to hear the messages for her. She didn't relate to anything I was saying. Here came the ego again, "what made you think you could do this?"

Then I heard a very soft whisper, "Keep going." Before the hour was up the lady had remembered things from her past that validated the message I had given her. The person coming through was an ex-boyfriend. It was as she put it a very abusive relationship and she hadn't thought of him in years. She had no idea he had crossed over. He came through to apologize and ask for forgiveness. When we came to the end of the session the Angel card for her was "New Beginnings and Fresh Starts." She laughed and said "I have a job opportunity and I have been trying to decide if I should take it. It would require me to relocate. I don't want to leave everything I know. But lately, I have felt this might be just what I need." She already knew the answer this card was simply a confirmation for her. The message on the card resonated with her and was what she needed to hear!

My heart sang, I could hear messages for others!

The next two weeks there were no clients booked, due to the skepticism of people in the small town I lived in there weren't too many people interested in having a reading. Annette and I agreed that I would go to the shop once a month instead of weekly.

Cindy was in charge of the company website, she asked me for an article to post on myself and what I do. She said, "There's a man I've heard about that does what you do. He has a website," as she was talking she was searching on the computer for the site. Once she found it, she wrote it down and handed me the piece of paper as she said, "Why don't you take a look at it and write something for me to post on our site."

That night as I read his website I discovered he was giving a two-day workshop the following month on Communicating with the Archangels. The thought ran through my mind *Pay attention to the signs. Jesus told me a good man was coming to teach me many things. Margo had mentioned to me about a man that talked to the Angels and now Cindy referred to this same man. Coincidence, no way this has to be the man, this had to be a confirmation? WOW!*

A wave of energy rushed through me, and I was on a high as I signed up for the workshop and made an appointment with him for a session. He was booked a month out, and his clients had given him fantastic reviews; my anticipation was growing as I just knew Spirit had led me to study under this man.

Meeting the Good Man

 With enthusiasm, I got up at 7:00 AM, on that June morning. Class started at 10:00 AM, I didn't want to be late. Jesus told me this man would teach me many things, and I was curious and eager to meet him.

When I got there, I was thankful it was a small group of about ten people. The energy in his home and the class of like minds was so inviting. Scott ten years my senior, with his salt and pepper hair and angelic blue eyes had the most loving energy about him. During his introduction, he told the story of when he began to hear voices. We all laughed as we understood the uncertainty of feeling, "Am I crazy? Is this real?" Then in his search for answers some twenty years ago

183

he went to California and took the Angel Therapy Practitioner workshop with Doreen Virtue. Wow, I was giddy as I thought *I couldn't take the Angel Therapy Practitioner directly under her so Spirit brought a teacher that had!"* Her one-day workshop I took was with three hundred other people, but this felt different. It wasn't just on how to give readings. His workshop was made up of the Angel Therapy teachings and his studies and experiences over the years.

We had partner exercises giving Archangel Readings to each other, perhaps it was the smaller group. It was unbelievable! I had never experienced anything like this! Each of us working with the Archangel's individually within a group generated a very high energy. Oh, my goodness, it was intoxicating! That afternoon we concluded the day with a group meditation, I had never been to a group meditation, so again this was exhilarating to me.

After the meditation was closed, Scott asked that we share what we experienced. As he went around the room and I listened to everyone, I knew which Archangel had appeared to them based on the color they saw. When it came to my turn, I was a little hesitant to speak my mind because what I saw was a brilliant purple swirling around, but something else happened.

I explained, "When we started down the hallway my mind filled with white light. I kept going down the hall, and the most amazing colors of green, blue, pink and purple swirled around me. I was floating through the colors, but it felt as if they were guiding me. When I opened my door, I saw a brilliant amethyst purple glow; I knew it was Archangel Zadkiel."

Scott smiled. I continued to explain what I saw and heard, "Then again the green, pink and blue swirled in and out but the purple was continuous. Then I heard a faint voice whisper *'Catalina.'* When you started guiding us out of the meditation, I turned to close the door behind me and again heard the faint whisper, *'Catalina.'*"

As I assumed, we were all connecting to Archangel's, and I had studied everything I could find on them. There was nothing mentioned of an Archangel Catalina in anything I read. Although I did understand that there are perhaps thousands of Archangels and currently only a few that work with humankind.

Some people giggled when I admitted, "I hadn't heard of an Archangel Catalina. I hadn't read anything about that one."

Comments around the room were meant to be humorous, "There's a Catalina salad dressing and Catalina Island." I looked to Scott who sat there with his pendulum in hand. I watched as he connected with Spirit.

I knew he asked a question, and I watched as his pendulum began to spin in a circle, whatever he asked he was receiving a confirmation. He looked at me and said, "I think you just met one of your guardian angels."

The room went silent, and without skipping a beat for any further conversation, he asked the next person to share their experience.

After class, he told me, "I asked Archangel Michael who Catalina was, and heard *'guardian angel.'* Then I asked, "Is Catalina one of Dianne's guardian angels?" and the pendulum confirmed the answer was yes.

I was jazzed, and I couldn't wait for the next class!

On the drive home, I called Ginger to explain everything we went over in class, and the meditation and the fact that Archangel Michael confirmed I had just met one of my guardian angels. As I was telling her, I had an electrifying AH'HA moment of confirmation. I glanced to the right lane as an RV passed me when I noticed across the back was the name, Catalina!

I exclaimed, "Oh my lord!"

Ginger asked, "What? Are you alright?"

I started laughing as I answered, "You aren't going to believe this!"

When I told her, what had just happened, all she could say was, "Wow." She laughed, and said what had become one of our favorite sayings for unexplainable events, "Spirit at work!"

Later that evening I was scrolling down my FB homepage when an ad for Catalina Island floated across the screen. Erie... Chills ran down my spine. This was the third confirmation of the name Catalina in one day. I had been asking for some time to hear my Guardian Angles name and Catalina wanted me to understand she was my Guardian Angel. I had heard from other people and read that it was rare that a Guardian Angel gave their name. I was excited as anyone would be.

You don't have to know names to call on the Archangel's or Angels. They are God's messengers, and they hear us when we ask for help. Perhaps wanting to know their names is a human thought, or it's just me, I find it much more real and personal. For me, it's like talking to an old friend or a close family member versus talking to a stranger. I began calling to her by name that night, and in my heart and mind, our relationship grew.

We have all had amazing experiences that we write off as crazy, spooky, or unexplainable because our intellectual mind can't find an explanation for it. Has the thought ever occurred to you that this is the Spirit world connecting with you?

I went to my first session after the initial class with Scott. My awareness and growth had all happened so quickly I was still in denial about my spiritual gifts I felt I needed answers. Deep within I also felt I had so much to learn, and I needed confirmations that what I heard and somehow knew was real.

My intention for the session was to receive anything Spirit wanted me to know. It was mind-blowing as I asked questions and Scott would give me the answer's he heard from Archangel Michael.

Scott began the session with a prayer then he sat and listened to the messages he was receiving. He looked up and smiled then said, "Archangel Michael is telling me you are an Old Indigo Soul and this is your 1800 lifetime here."

I light-heartedly replied, "Damn I look good for my age!"

Scott laughed at my comment then began to tell me, "I am hearing that your first incarnation was in Atlantis where you were a Healer."

Ah I thought, *that explains a few things.* **Healing and Atlantis!**

"That explains my knowing with Atlantis!" I replied with elation.

Since I was a child I had pictured a world such as Atlantis. Everything I had read about Atlantis spoke to my soul. I could see it in my mind. What I saw was a utopia, a civilization of peace and harmony for the betterment of humankind. I could picture it in my mind, the world I so desired. Now I discovered that I did live there, was that why I could see it so clearly? I belonged to this friendly society at one time, until eventually; the free will of humankind destroyed it.

I began to tell him, "During the class when you guided us on the Atlantis Meditation I felt so at home like I had been there. I rode that dolphin, and I knew every inch of that waterway. Wow!"

He again smiled at my excitement. "Michael is saying they called you Shanta Belladonna."

Okay, now he had my attention!

"WOW!" I exclaimed, "You aren't going to believe this, my writing partner Ginger and I just released our first book in a series. One of the main characters is named Ashanti."

He smiled, and I said, "No that's not all. I recently researched and introduced the Belladonna plant into the second book."

I was overwhelmed at the confirmations I was given. We were both in a state of utter glee, after all, the energy of happiness and excitement is contagious.

The first half of our session came to a close as I told him that I had drawn a card, "Make a Wish."

Scott commented, "Nice," then asked, "What did you wish for?"

I answered, "I asked God to please let me see his Angels'."

He smiled at me, and from the look on his face and the way he tilted his head slightly upward, I knew he was listening to Archangel Michael answers.

Scott led me over to a healing bed he had created with the Archangel Raphael. I had heard about the "John of God Bed," but never had an opportunity to attend any of his sessions. I was excited to experience whatever spirit had in store for me.

Once I was comfortable, he began with a guided meditation as he played the crystal bowls. I drifted away, higher and higher. There were the most brilliant colors, deeper hues than I had ever seen on the color spectrum. I drifted in the magnificent sea of blues, greens, purples, gold, and pinks. They reminded me of vapor or mist. The colors surrounded me as they weaved in and out of my vision when I saw the opening of a cave. At the mouth stood the white wolf, I entered and followed the wolf. When we got to the heart of the cave there were other animals; I noticed a black panther, dolphin, snake, bear, hawk and many others surrounding and watching. The white wolf stood beside me.

Back on this plane, I felt I was drifting on a cloud; I couldn't feel my body. I was a feather. In the meditation, suddenly I saw a golden light coming toward me. When I looked across the cave, I recognized the face of Jesus.

I ran to him and fell to my knees. I bowed my head and began to weep uncontrollably. I felt his gentle touch as he raised me up and softly lifted my chin. I was looking into the most alluring amber eyes I had ever seen. We bonded on a soul level through time and space we were united.

"I am so sorry it took me so long to get here." As if I knew he was expecting me and I was running late. I wasn't speaking with my voice, rather through my heart.

He wrapped me in his embrace. It was the most peaceful love I had ever felt. He smiled down at me whispering in my ear, "I have always been here waiting."

This embrace lasted probably no more than a moment when the colors began to come in again, and then whoosh he was gone.

Once the session was over, I lingered a moment and wiped the tears from my eyes. At a loss for words, I asked Scott, "Did you see the White Wolf?"

Scott handed me a Kleenex and a glass of water, as he replied, "Yes, but not at first. I wondered why the panther didn't come near you and then I saw the wolf. I also saw the dolphin, I've never seen a dolphin in a cave," he winked.

We both chuckled.

I blew my nose and then gently remarked, "Jesus came."

He replied, "Yes," as he opened the blinds and helped me off the table.

Something in me knew he didn't see or feel what I experienced; this was a private moment held just for me with no explanation needed. I moved back over to the chair, and I began to describe the colors. I was in awe of their brilliance.

Scott grinned and said, "I think you just got your wish."

"What wish?" For a brief moment, I wasn't thinking straight. Then I remembered, "Oh Wow! Really, the colors are how I see the Angels?" I questioned.

He explained, "Most see the halo color of the Angel's and their energies. Actually when people say 'I see the Angels,' they mean the Angels halo glow.

"All this time I have been expecting when I finally saw an Angel it would be standing in front of me. I have been seeing Angel's the way I see Angel's for some time through their colors."

He shook his head yes and said, "When you told me about your wish, Michael laughed and said 'she see's us.'"

My thoughts; "*Why hasn't anyone told me that when they say I see Angels, they saw their halo colors?" When they come into my mind's eye, I know who they are by their halo colors. I greet them by name. I thought people meant they saw an Angel standing in front of them, live, outside their heads and I wanted to see them too!*

I had just received confirmation that I had seen Archangels and at that moment I heard the chuckles in heaven at my thought.

On the drive home, I smiled as I thought about the visit with Jesus. Why was this time so emotional? I had visited him in my dream world, and meditations previously. Something changed. 🖋

I signed up for the second workshop Scott offered. This one on Mediumship scheduled for the following month and Ginger decided to go with me.

During one of the exercises, that day is when I learned about the gatekeeper. We sat quietly and listened, then wrote down any names we heard in our minds. Next, we were to acknowledge the spirit and the messages they gave us for one of the students; it enabled us to identify the souls who had crossed over. These would-be spirits that were associated with the students in the class. The spirits are called Deceased Loved Ones and could be family, friends or pets. As the names were read, we discovered how many of us had heard the same name. Then who knew a person by that name. If more than one student knew someone by that name, it was then a process of elimination through the details received as to whose deceased loved one was there with us.

We went around the room and took turns reading our list of names. Ginger read her list, when she said Alton. I was the only other person that also had Alton on my list.

Neither I nor anyone else recalled having a deceased loved one by that name when I heard a whisper, "Neighbor."

Oh, my goodness "Alton was an acquaintance, he and his wife lived across the street from us, but moved out of the neighborhood ten years ago. He had pancreatic cancer and died a year after they moved. I didn't know him very well."

Ginger said, "I can't understand everything he's saying, but he said something about his wife and a book."

"I don't know how to get a hold of her." I replied, when I heard, "Nancy."

How odd! Alton's sister Nancy was the wife of one of Mark's boating friends.

Scott began to explain the importance of a Gatekeeper. Simply put, it is hiring a spiritual light being who will only allow others through when you invite them. As demonstrated in this exercise when the gate is open anyone in the spiritual realm not only deceased loved ones, can communicate with you. Anyone also meant dark forces as well.

I honestly didn't think much about Alton showing up in class. However, Alton was on a mission. He was persistent and visited me that night and the next morning. In talking with him, it turned out the book which I saw in my minds' eye was a Family Bible. He explained that he wanted the Bible to be passed down to his younger brother. He also mentioned a letter that he had written to be delivered. I understood Alton wanted his message to be heard, and I wasn't sure how but I would try. I didn't know if his family was open to hearing what he had to say.

Mark and I were on our way to run errands when I asked, "Can we go by Nancy and Ned's house? I need to give her this message if she is open to hearing it. I don't think Alton is going to leave me alone until I do."

"Huh? Yea, I guess," he said apprehensively. He knew if he didn't stop by their house, I would go on my own later because I was on a mission to deliver this information.

193

I explained the story to Nancy, ending with the question "If you are open and would like to receive his message I would be happy to give it to you."

Nancy said, "Sure," and when I finished, she said, "Wow," she explained that Alton was her half brother, they had the same mother, and the brother was from his dad's previous marriage. She also said she and Flo, Alton's wife didn't get along and hadn't kept in contact. "The Bible belonged to his dad's family. I don't know where it is, but what you are telling me it belongs to his brother. I bet Flo's daughter has it. I don't know anything about a letter. Flo lives on the other side of the lake, but I'm not sure where. Flo and I weren't that close, but you've got to tell Ned, he and Alton were best friends, and he misses him so much.

I went outside and talked with Ned and Alton came through for him. It was to me a beautiful confirmation for Ned that loved ones are always with us. However, I was still concerned about the Bible. We left and continued on our errands, as we approached a convenience market, I asked Mark to pull in so that I could get a bottle of water.

As I entered, Flo walked toward the exit. *Flo,* I was in awe; Divine Timing was at work.

I walked up and greeted Flo. I began to share the entire episode with her. I think she was in shock, but when I asked if she would like to hear the message. She answered "Yes." Then I told her about Alton and the bible, the brother, the letter, etc.

With a tearful voice, she explained that her daughter had the Bible. After Alton had died, and they found it, they had tried

194

to give it to Alton's brother, but he moved after the funeral, and no one knew where he was. Alton died during their daughter's pregnancy. He had written a letter to his grandson before he died. The letter was Alton's way of introducing himself to him. To tell him how sorry he was that he would miss out on sharing so many of life's little pleasures with him. Such as baseball, fishing and teaching him to water ski, things as she put it that grandpa's do with their grandsons, and to say I Love You. The boy was at this time nine. She and her daughter had recently discussed when would be the right time to give him the letter and this was Flo's confirmation that it was time.

Cherub

Hiring a gatekeeper is just as it sounds; someone to guard the gate, keeping Spiritual beings away from you unless you invite them to come. In reality, it is evading your Free Will for them to pop in when you don't want to hear them. Wow! No wonder I could hear others loved ones even when I didn't want them there. Friends, family, and stranger's I walked by in the grocery store, or on the sidewalk. They are all around us, and when you acknowledge that you hear them in any mmm! way then they just keep talking. I also had the thought that it is also evading others Free Will if you give them a message that they have not asked to receive. ???

After the event with Alton, I asked Archangel Michael to be my gatekeeper. It wasn't until several weeks later that I realized once again I wasn't clear with my words. I stopped hearing my loved ones for several weeks. I knew they could only visit one person at a time, but it was unusual not to hear from any of them. I asked Archangel Michael, "Why haven't I heard them?" One word entered my mind, "Gatekeeper."

195

With that, I knew what I should do. "Archangel Michael, I ask you to be my gatekeeper, allowing only Divine Intelligence and my loved ones through, unless I ask for someone else and then allowing loving healing messages for others."

Spirit is Awesome!

It was that summer I realized my life had gone through many changes. Old friends and I no longer shared the same interest, and they slowly dirtied away. I desired friends that understood my new interest. I prayed for and craved like-minded people that shared and discussed Spirituality and beliefs.

My family loved me, and they accepted the new me, because of that love.

In a conversation with Mark I tried to explain the joy in my heart. "I just want everyone to feel this joy and love that I feel. I know in my every being that God has given all of us the ability to connect with the Heavenly Realm. We are all loved so much and I want to share that with the world."

I was surprised at his response, "I don't understand what you do, but you are an intelligent woman so I do know that if you believe it then there is something to it."

That was the sweetest thing he could have ever said to me as I knew all the doubts he had. I continued to talk with my family about the love of God, Jesus, the Archangels and connecting with that love. It was actually comical to me why Mark didn't think they could hear him.

I don't recall the request but the incident lingers in my mind, one day he said, "Ask your angels_____."

I laughed as I walked into the house, "You ask them, they are just waiting to talk to you."

It was a few minutes later he came in and I asked, "So did you ask Archangel Michael?"

Jokingly he answered, "Nope, my angels name is Voltron."

Immediately I heard Michaels' little snicker, "I go by many names."

Ginger and I had talked numerous times over the last year about starting up a monthly Spiritual Group, I had mentioned it to Margo at "This Rocks and Glitter's, "and she was enthusiastic about the idea of hosting the gatherings in her shop.

One morning late June I pulled my cards for the day. There was one card which in short told me to put a fire under my butt and get on with it. I was watering my garden as I asked, "I have so many ideas which one is it that I need to get on with?"

When I heard, "Pick a date!"

Pick a date? I thought. Then I heard, "like minds."

 I laughed, and said, "Thank You, Archangel Uriel."

I went in the house and turned the calendar to July. I closed my eyes and pointed, when I opened them my finger was on July 26. I called Margo and Ginger to confirm that July 26 was okay with them. Our first Spiritual Gathering was scheduled.

To my surprise a dozen people attended. We introduced Angel Readings to the group which led to Margo asking Ginger and me to give readings out of her shop every Friday.

I explained this to Annette, and she agreed I should make the change, all things work in Divine Timing. I am forever grateful to Annette for providing me the opportunity to step out of the Spiritual Closet.

As the summer of 2014 marched on it proved to be a busy one. Ginger and I were promoting The Balance: Awakenings, in Houston, Galveston, Austin, San Antonio and our local area. The monthly Spiritual Gatherings were growing, and I was working at the shop every other Friday. I attended three additional classes with Scott and continued my one-on-one mentorship session's monthly, and my dream world was full of messages.

"Choose a Healing Modality," Began to show up for me in my oracle card for the day. Again, Spirit was leading me back to healing.

I woke up one morning and read my notes from my dream world, "Selenite grid." I had previously received the message, and it was my practice to circle myself and the client with a grid of crystals. But, what was Selenite?

I asked the dream cards, "What was the message in my dream telling me?" As I shuffled the cards, the Selenite card flew out of the deck face up. Spiritual Activation, now I understood the words, "build a grid with Selenite and Spirit will come." This was wild!

For the next two days, I studied everything I could find on Selenite and found it to be a stone used for clearing negative energies. Some call it an Archangel Michael stone and make swords out of it to cleanse and balance the chakra's (energy centers in the body.) Others call it the SOS of crystals, as it is said to dissolve all negativity and protect everything in its area. It does not absorb the negative energy but dissolves it. *Hmm,* I thought *it must work, or Spirit wouldn't have brought the message to me.*

I knew I had to have Selenite; otherwise, it wouldn't have come to me in my dream world. I called Margo she was out that day but her husband Tim said they had a few pieces.

The next morning, I went to the shop when I walked in Margo looked up and said, "Hey you, I heard you were coming in today. You called about Selenite?"

I answered, "Yes."

She stood up and said, "Follow me," we walked across to the far corner of the shop. She bent down and picked up a small piece out of a basket, handing it to me she said, "It was dirty when I got it. I tried to clean it with olive oil."

The stone felt oily and was dingy looking. As I looked at it, I wasn't excited about this piece of Selenite. I quietly said, "Oh," in a disappointed tone.

I handed it back to Margo. She looked at me and said, "Now follow me and let me show you what came in today."

We walked to the other side of the shop, and I followed her to the storage area. She stopped and pointed to the floor. The aisle was lined with big beautiful pieces of Selenite.

She laughed jokingly, "Honey, you've got some connections! My rock vendor came this morning, and this Selenite was on his truck." She swept her hand downward motioning to the most beautiful Selenite slabs. She shook her head, and we both laughed. Then the hair on our arms stood up. Angel Bumps!

I answered, "Spirit at Work!"

Energy Healing

Now that I had Selenite, I knew how to build a grid, and the dreams kept coming. I pondered how to do energy healing. One afternoon we were sitting on the porch, I looked at Ginger and said, "Okay, I need a guinea pig, I don't know what I'm doing, but Spirit keeps showing me and sending me messages about being a Healer."

Ginger is a Reiki Master, and she understood what I was asking of her.

"Okay, of course," She said, and added, "My lower back has been bothering me for days, so I'm game!"

"I'd like to try, even if I'm not 100% sure if I can."

Without hesitation, she answered, "Okay let's do it."

I didn't have a clue, but I had to try. We went upstairs where I built the Selenite grid, and began my first energy healing session intuitively. I asked, and I was guided how to move my hands in a heart shape motion. Then I moved my hands to the area's I was led, I just knew where to direct the energy and I felt heat coming through me. I heard "lower back," and moved over her lower back as I repeated the heart shape outline with my hands. Next, I was guided to the knees, when I heard "pull her legs, straighten the spine." I grabbed her ankles and gently pulled. It was the most amazing experience for me.

When we (Spirit and I) finished the session, I felt the energy fading and knew the session was over.

She said, "I felt the energy from your hands coming through my clothes! Your hands generated a heat."

I explained what I experienced. "I was so warm and tingly, and then I started sweating from the heat. Spirit was teaching me, I could hear them and I just followed. "Move your hands clock wise starting at the crown and work down the body." As I did, I was completely blown away by the energy I felt flowing through me, the energy from God.

In the next month, I did a session a week on her. I heard and was guided by Archangel Raphael what and how to do this. I used a Selenite grid and had purchased Selenite wand's to help in the healing process. I would get information where to touch certain parts of the body." I did as I was guided as God's conduit.

It was incredible! I trusted, and Spirit delivered.

Mark came home during this time, and he had pulled his shoulder muscle and it had become very bothersome to him.

One evening I asked, "Would you like for me to do some energy healing on that shoulder?"

He asked, "How do you do?"

I explained, "I listen and move my hands over some parts of the body to direct the energy. Sometimes I am guided to certain areas of the body; it's just a knowing."

With hesitation, he said, "Okay, anything for relief."

I mentioned to him during this session that performing the healing while bending over the bed was killing my back.

What a sweet loving man I married. Within a few days, a massage table was delivered.

This was mind blowing to me and I wanted to know more; I wanted to understand the principals of Energy Healing work. I found an online Reiki Course, and to my astonishment the instructor Betty had also studied under Scott and used one of his Healing Table in her practice. I took this as a sign from Spirit and registered!

I had unusual experiences with the Reiki attunements. Betty would tell me when she was going to send me the energy attunement. I would sit very quietly with my eyes closed. Next what I have come to call a metal helmet was placed over my head gradually. I felt the weight over the top of my crown, and it extended down past my third eye. At the close of the energy, I saw a beautiful purple winged Angel, which I was told was the Angel of Reiki. Once I completed Level One and Two, I did my internship with three friends. After the session I interviewed the person by asking them to explain their experiences. Each commented on the feeling of floating, the feeling of peace and each saw lights floating around them. As I was delivering the energy, I was receiving messages for them some from Jesus, the Archangels and Deceased Loved Ones all coming through loud and clear. I was now receiving information during the Energy Healing for a combined Healing Intuitive session.

After my internship, Betty asked if I was interested in going to the Master Level. I explained to her that I had taken the course to understand the principles of Reiki and Energy Healing. I heard and was guided by Spirit intuitively on the hand movements and areas of the body which needed the energy.

She understood and then said, "I heard a message for you during your attunement; the Angels asked that I tell you 'we need more Mystic Intuitive Healers.'" I did try using just the Reiki a few times, but it wasn't the same as the Healing I was doing prior. Nothing against it as I have had beautiful Reiki sessions myself, it just didn't feel right for me.

A few weeks later I went to see Scott for my Spiritual Checkup, what I now called my monthly sessions with him. As I was leaving, he said, "The Angels are asking me to tell you not to change what you are doing in your healing work."

Confirmation received.

I often heard the words from my previous dream, "Walk through the color for healing," I began to search to discover how I could incorporate color into the sessions. I found a light that had all of the chakra colors. I realized with each client Spirit would give me a list of crystals to be used, Smokey Quartz, Rose Quartz, Clear Quartz, and Amethyst to name a few, all set up and surrounded by the Selenite grid. Sometimes they were placed the same, but other times they would be slightly different. I soon realized the crystals I was using were the stones of the Archangel's. I began building grids under the table based on where I heard to place them. I heard messages from the Spiritual Realm during the sessions. The Healing Bed was similar to Scott's but yet different; I was the conduit for healing. I would later be led to call it Crystal Intuitive Angelic Healing.

October of 2014 a beautiful fall afternoon while driving I asked, "Archangel Michael who else wishes to work with me?"

I heard the name "Nathaniel."

"There's no Archangel Nathaniel," I mumbled; "hmm." Then the memory of my Uncle Nathaniel, who passed on when I was child, entered my thoughts. I wasn't sure why as we weren't close. But knowing our loved ones are always around us, and considering I was in an awareness state, I thanked him, and never gave this a second thought.

CHAPTER 16
Spirit Burst!

Spirit speaks to me like the rush of the wind. One rainy October day while I sat on the porch and listened I heard, "Teach them in the masses."

I laughed, "Come on how am I to do that?"

That night while searching for an event online, I ran across a Spiritual Newsletter, as I was reading I heard, "newsletter."

Over the next couple of days "newsletter" entered my mind many times. I laughed and asked, "Okay, what shall we call it?

"Spirit Burst," this time with a giggle.

Not the first time I had heard this term, I had to laugh as I realized Spirit is always planting seeds for later growth. Angels are awe-inspiring helpers, and friends, when we ask for help, they are always there.

Daily Spiritual Maintenance

There is one message that I am being asked to share with you in these writings. Spiritual Health, what I lovingly named "Daily Spiritual Maintenance."

I hear and read of Lightworker's feeling disconnected, being scattered, feeling drained, feeling all kinds of crazy energies. Periods of disconnection remains a hot topic among my friends and on social media.

My question in 2015, "Archangel Michael, each teacher I have studied with always mentions, 'you are sensitive to energy, you must clear and ground yourself, and you must protect your energy.' What message should I share with others on the importance of Spiritual Health?"

Here is the Spirit Burst from the loving Archangel Michael.

"I greet you this day, beloved brothers and sisters of the earth to speak of your Spiritual Health through this beloved lightworker. Lightworker's you are Very sensitive to all the energies around you and the world. Why then aren't you practicing Daily maintenance? You are sensitive to your environment, and absorb energies. Are you not aware that doing kind deeds for someone you form a cord of attachment, which allows you to pick up their energies? There are also dark forces all around you that wish to feed off of your light. Even your media brings forth energies of sadness, energies of chaos, energies of fear. Chaos and Fear are Lower Energies, Negative Energies. You're like sponges soaking up these energies. The practices we bring forth to you aren't something you do once and set for this lifetime. Nor do you do them only when you feel they are needed. You eat daily, some pray daily, why then haven't you developed your daily maintenance for your Spiritual Health? You all have much work to do on earth, and we ask that you take care of self to be of Creators' serve to others. We are family, I am your brother and care deeply for each of you, it is my honor to guide and protect each one of you. Love yourself in the way Creator loves you. Love yourself enough to practice good Spiritual Health."

For me, in our chaotic times these practices should be done at least twice a day, and up until this conversation with Michael, I only asked to be cleared and protected when I felt the need.

1-7 July

7 oranges

Play like ball

Ps 72

drink early morning

(4) seven days

(moko bhi di eranlbode)

2018 430048

M

... school division

Doctor — Panny Fazeelat

Clinic — Southtown medical clinic

Weight — 63 kg

Height — 164 cm

SIN — 687 882 472

Contigent owner —

Beneficiary Primary —

Financial Income —

Email address — @motolasolomon@gmail.com

Trustee

Bank — 03687-5019302

employer — pension details

Sin

Clinic —

wages/leect

Can't get over

benefacia nes

financial income

—

Bank — 03687-5019302

* Bank — 03687 -5019302
* Employer — Pembina Trails Sch. division
* Doctor — Pannu Fazeelat
* clinic — Southtown medical clinic
* weight — 63 kg
* Height — 164 cm
* SIN — 687882 472
* Email — omotolasolomon@gmail.com

* Beneficary — Ibukun, Ayomide, Tomiwa
* Financial Income 24,000

office2otis@gmail.com

In another conversation, I asked "Michael you know we live in a world that is also sensitive to time issues. There are days that if I am running late for an appointment and don't make time for the maintenance. What can I do?"

The answer was simple, which equated to, "Hire a Spiritual Maintenance Team!"

Dah! How simple can that be? ASK, that's all it takes is for you to ASK!

Spirit at Work Once Again

One afternoon in early November 2014 I was reading on the metaphysical fairs in Austin. When I thought *there has to be a metaphysical festival in the San Antonio area. I would love to work a festival doing Angel Readings and Energy Work.*

I began to search and finally found one, and it was to be held the next weekend. How exciting, I called Ginger and invited her to go with me to check it out. After I hung up with her, I thought *I'll send the Organizer an email for the info to work the event.*

When I heard in my head, "Perhaps you should call."

"Oh, there is probably a waiting list. I'll just email the organizer." I replied back to Spirit.

"It would behoove you to make a call."

Muttering to Spirit I picked up the phone to key in the number. As it rang, I was honestly expecting to leave my inquiry on a recording.

On the third ring, I heard, "Hello this is Tina, can I help you?"

After a few minutes of conversation, she said, "This is most definitely a Spirit thing, I never have cancellations, and I just had one, how would you like to start this weekend?"

I explained I had a writing partner and we would like to sell our book there. Then I said, "We both work with the Angels and give readings and healing. Could we share a table?

"Oh yes, we'd love it!" She answered enthusiastically.

I hung up in glee as I called Ginger, I couldn't hold my excitement, "Well, instead of attending the festival, how would you like to be a vendor?"

"What, how?" I explained my two conversations, one with Spirit and one with Tina.

In Unisom, we said, "Spirit at Work!"

Angel Navigation LLC

Through the end of 2014, I received the same message repeatedly in my dream world, "You are being called to teach." I awoke one morning and noticed I had written something down that night. When I read it, I understood. "Teach them to connect. We will do the rest."

This message resonated with everything inside of me. I had been teaching others in my day to day conversations, by explaining that we all connect, telling of God's heavenly messengers. I would give them the name of the Archangel that could help them with a given situation. Yes, teach others how to find their Connection and the Archangels.

Then I thought, *maybe I can teach at the festival once a month.*

I wasn't sure what was next but I followed my intuition and January 2015, Angel Navigation LLC was born and I began teaching out of my home.

CHAPTER 17
My Spiritual Birthday Party

Now January 2015 and for two weeks I proclaimed, I am having a Spiritual Birthday party. I invited God, Jesus, Archangel's, Angel's, Ascended Masters, Fairies, my deceased loved ones, and ancient ancestors. I welcomed all heavenly light beings and loved ones that wanted to attend. I had booked an appointment with Scott on the Healing Table as my birthday gift to myself, being my fifty-eighth birthday and the number broken down is four, the number for the Angels; I wanted to have a big Spiritual celebration.

A few days before, I was talking with my Mom and asked if she was going to be able to be at my party.

"But of course," she answered. "We're making you a cake!"

My tears pooled as I saw in my mind's eye a beautiful ivory cake with white pearls and on the top, it had the most compelling bluish flame, representing a candle. It stood at least 50 feet tall. It was by far the largest cake I had ever seen.

"Oh mom," I said, as I sat there silently weeping and missing her, I knew she was with me, but I hadn't outgrown the need for the hug of my mom.

I heard her say, "I love you, but I must go, there's so much to do."

I felt a soft touch across my cheek, a kiss and then poof she vanished.

Two days later on my birthday, I got up with excitement knowing I'd be having a spiritual birthday.

I talked to Spirit the entire way to Scott's. I was giddy. I got out and walked to the door and said to the Spiritual Realm, "Are ya'll ready?" Which was met with a gentle laugh, and then I heard, "Are you?"

Scott opened the door before I could ring the bell, with a gigantic smile on his face and a thrill in his voice, he said, "Wow you brought a whole team with you." Laughingly he invited us in.

In his office, I said, "Today is my birthday, and I am having a Spiritual Birthday party. That's why they're all here."

He laughed and replied, "Well, let's get started as he shut the blinds and I made myself comfortable on the Healing Table. He began the guided meditation followed by the crystal bowls. This time I was aboard Archangel Michael's Purple Pyramid. As I stepped into the pyramid, Archangel Michael greeted me with a smile and then said, "You may invite any light beings you wish to join us."

Who to ask? But as I thought of a name their spirit appeared; Jesus, Saint Germaine, Mother Mary, Saint Francis, Archangel's and my Guardian Angel.

As the pyramid was lifted higher and higher leaving the earth behind a thrill of excitement ran through me. I looked out the window as the earth got smaller and smaller. I watched as we passed other planets. As we approached a brilliant blue planet, I felt the warm blanket of love wrap around me, and I had the overwhelming feeling that I had been there before. Out the window, I noticed what looked to be a space docking station. As we got closer I heard the heavenly choir, it was an exquisite melody as they serenaded our arrival.

Once the pyramid unfolded, I stepped out on the platform which overlooked thousands of people. They were cheering, and the feeling of unequivocal compassion surrounded me, I felt Pure Love, Total Acceptance, Belonging, The Unconditional Love of God wrapped me, embraced me and I was home.

As I stood there, my heart was full, and then I was what I would describe as crowd surfing. In total trust, I fell back into the crowd of souls. I was being lifted up and touched by beauty and light. I had the feeling that I knew all of these beautiful souls who loved me and welcomed me home. I had never felt so loved, and I wasn't afraid; on the contrary, I was full of joy, as the energy of love ran through me. I was safe, as I surfed through the crowd of love. I felt the most peaceful feeling I had ever known. I watched as the Archangel's weaved in and out and around me as I flew higher and higher out of my physical body.

Meanwhile back in this realm, the session was ending, as I heard Scott say "it's time to board Michael's Purple Pyramid for your journey back to earth." I was having too much fun, and I didn't want to go. Someone was holding my knees, and I couldn't move; at that moment I knew it was time to go, I waved goodbye and stepped into the pyramid. The Archangel's surrounded me, embarrassed me as they wrapped me in a quilt of their brilliant colors.

I looked out, and we were getting closer and closer to earth. The next thing I knew I was back on the table. My first thought was Wow! What a marvelous experience that was!

I slowly got off the table and made my way to the chair for grounding.

I asked, "Where was I?"

Scott answered with utter glee, "Venus, the planet of Love, and Thank You for the Love Fest."

We were both smiling, "Did you see all the souls there?" I asked.

"Your ancient ancestors," he replied. "There were thousands!"

"Yes, I could feel them. I saw a sea of souls, they were light, all shining.

In excitement, Scott asked, "Did you see that cake?"

"No, I was too wrapped in the feelings of Love."

He said, "It was the largest cake I have ever seen, multi-stories high! It was Ivory, with white pearls, and blue energy that looked like flames."

I was still floating, as I answered, "I didn't see it today, but that's actually what I saw when my mom said they were making me a cake. Wow, Scott! That was the most remarkable experience!" I took a sip of water. "I felt like someone was holding my knees down."

He said, "Yes, they were holding the Golden Cords to keep you connected to your body because your soul was high above you."

I took another sip of water, "I don't know how to explain it, I wanted to stay there. It felt like home."

He grinned, "I compare it to being on vacation. You leave the day to day stress behind for a while, you're having so much fun; but when it's time to return home, you know you have to go."

"Yes my sentiments exactly!" I exclaimed.

On the drive home, I was in conversation with God, thanking him and all who attended my birthday celebration. Then I said, "Mama, Daddy, Bubba, I didn't see you there, but then again, I didn't see any faces, it was just a knowing."

At that moment, the song that reminds me of Bubba came on the radio. As I drove and cried and sang "I Can Only Imagine," I knew that was a confirmation that they were all there, I had visited the heavenly realm and my heart was bursting with bliss.

An average hour and twenty-five-minute drive took me two and a half hours. I didn't know where I was going, driving down the country roads, making my way back home. I would turn, and the GPS would change course. Perhaps that was another sign, which it doesn't matter the path you choose, you'll ultimately end up at the destination.

The next day I was still flying, I called it my state of grace, there was nothing that could shake my feeling of being so connected to Spirit.

I got dressed and went to do a few errands; knowing I still had to function in the earthly realm. About an hour later I decided I would go home and finish later; I needed a little more grounding.

That afternoon after a grounding meditation, I went out to finish my errands. Last stop the grocery store. When I walked in, I saw an elderly lady friend. She looked up, and we greeted each other she remarked, "Honey you are glowing."

I laughed and said, "Spirit in my heart and it's full of love and compassion."

Then I heard, "tell her about your celebration."

I began by telling her, "I had the most wonderful birthday gift from God."

As I described it to her, she had a look of trust and faith in her eyes, and she too was glowing.

Love was shining through her eyes as she asked, "Is that for all of us?"

I smiled as the joy burst from me and replied, "Oh yes, oh yes, it's more love than you could imagine."

She hugged me and softly said, "I am ninety-two years old, and I so needed to hear that today."

We stood in an embrace, one heart sharing the love with another as we said our goodbyes, and I went on about my shopping.

I could have gone to the store earlier when I was out. However, I followed my intuition and went later in the day. My thoughts, Spirit knew she was going to be there later in the day, she needed to hear the story, and by the way, her name is Grace.

Teaching

I began working with the Archangel Gabriel in December to form an outline and research as we put the workshop together to help others understand and open to their connection.

Beginning with everything being energy and connecting through what we know as clairs. Teach the students how to discover their connection and through interactive exercises, explore it. We (Spirit & I) would also give them tools to help strengthen their clair's. This would assist them to build confidence, and answer the question "No you aren't crazy, this is real and happening to you!" Giving a better understanding of how we are ALL CONNECTED to God, Source of All.

I had initially thought I would include The Archangel's. However, in conversation with Archangel Gabriel, I realized this would be far too much information to cover in a six-hour period, and concluded the Archangel's would be an additional workshop.

"Meet the Archangels" was planned for the spring, introducing the Archangel's and their specialties, with stories of my experiences in working with each of them.

On January 24, the first Angel Navigation Workshop "Connecting with Spirit" was held. The six-hour class was incredible; to see others light up when they made their connection with Spirit. The awe's in their eyes while participating in the interactive partner exercises. I cried as I watched them in meditation, my heart was soaring. I realized that was the joy of teaching. Tears of joy-filled my eyes and I knew then, at that moment, the answer to the card, "You are being called to teach."

I'm not sure who had more fun that day, the students, Spirit, or me! Thank You, Father-Mother God, Creator, Source of All, Jesus and the delightful emissaries.

Meeting Brandon

Spirit led me to yet another deep healing. While working at the monthly Spiritual Festival, I met Sophie. She was a petite, 4 ft 9 outspoken red headed Energy Healer and Intuitive. Sophie, a Reiki Master, had studied and practiced Eastern Medicine and embraced the culture and beliefs. This February Sunday was a rainy one and offered up a small crowd for the day. I watched her from across the way as she worked with clients and balanced their chakras. That afternoon I decided I would have a session with her.

She had me sit in a chair as she sat across from me she ran her hand over my aura. She smiled, bowed toward me as she sincerely said, "You are an old soul. It is an honor to meet you. I sense you do not allow many people to work with your energy. Thank you for trusting me."

She was right; I was aware that we absorb other's energy and very attuned to others. I was and am particular on who I allow to open my energy field. Sophie was the third Energy Healer I had felt comfortable to request a session.

As the session progressed, she said, "I feel a very young male soul with you.

I looked at her in bewilderment.

She then asked me, "What was the traumatic event that happened to you in your early twenties?"

I shook my head no, as to say "I don't remember," and responded, "I can't think of anything." As the words came out of my mouth, the scene in the hospital played through my mind. "I had a near death experience in my twenties."

"What happened?" I explained, "I went into labor during my sixth month of pregnancy and lost a baby boy." I noticed a slight smile in her eyes. "I had a near death experience during the delivery. I saw a white light, and a golden hand reached out to me. I lingered in the light and then choose not to take the hand and returned to my body."

That was thirty-six years ago. As soon as I began to talk about the loss, the wound opened and bled fresh, bright blood. After all, these years this was the first time I had voiced my grief, my sadness, my love and my guilt. Everything I had held inside bleed out of my heart. I felt this part of my heart had been locked and put away, and Sophie had just found the key and with Spirit she help unlocked the cage door and let it free. I sat there and balled my eyes out as I crumbled and released years of unmentioned, unspoken and unacknowledged feelings.

"Have you ever thought your soul had an agreement to escort him to the light? That it was a pack made before he was born?"

"No, I hadn't thought of that. It hurt so badly that I had stuffed the event deep inside. I never discussed it and rarely thought of it at all."

Sophie explained that she had learned that every soul chooses their life lessons each lifetime. In some cultures, they believe when a baby transcends, that this soul came in only to experience the womb. Then that soul's spirit goes on to be a Spirit Guide for someone in the family. She asked, "Did you give him a name?"

"Brandon," I answered tearfully.

Her next question took me aback, "Have you ever acknowledged that soul?"

At that moment, I began to shed even more tears as I answered, "No, I blocked the whole event out of my mind and closed my heart to it."

She smiled as she gently touched my hand, and replied, "You may have closed your heart to him, but he never closed his. He is with you now. Tell him how you feel."

"Brandon," as soon as I spoke his name my voice began to crack through my sobs as a rambled, "Please forgive me. I never knew how to express the emptiness I felt in losing you, it left a hole in my being." I wiped my tears, "I felt guilty; I thought it was my fault, I had to have done something wrong. I built a wall around that guilt and covered it up by not acknowledging you. If I didn't talk about the situation, then I didn't have to relive the feelings. I understand I made it all about me. I am sorry. I have always loved you, and I am sorry for not acknowledging you."

I heard his soft whisper in my ear, "mother," within seconds I felt his warmth wrap itself around me. I cried tears of love and loss for his soul all at the same time. I had begun a deep healing which was a long overdue.

That night I lit a candle for my son Brandon and thanked him for entering my life. Most nights I still burn a candle for him, and I sit and talk with him.

For years, I had buried the pain, but now I felt an ease with talking about him. Mark called the next day; I discussed Brandon with him. He knew I had lost a child, but that was all I had told him, this time I expressed my feelings. I also talked to my kids and acknowledged Brandon's soul, and I discovered they had always acknowledged him.

When asked, "How many children do you have?" My answer is, "Four total, three living."

It was later at Anne's home during a family event that the opportunity presented itself to discuss Brandon with Andrew.

I knew it was now time to say all the things that had gone unsaid that thirty plus years ago.

"I'd like to talk to you a minute. Can we go outside?"

As we walked to the back of the house, I said, "I wanted to talk about Brandon."

I caught him completely off guard.

"We never had a conversation about losing him; we had no service for him, no closure, and in my mind, it was like he never existed. I convinced myself that I hadn't formed a bond

220

with him. For all these years, I blamed myself for not having a healthy baby, and I carried guilt for so many years. Even though the doctors gave us medical reasons, I realize I somehow blamed myself. Because we never talked about it, I felt you blamed me as well."

A look of heartache came across his face, "I never blamed you, Dianne."

"Andrew I didn't know how to deal with it, so I didn't want to talk about him." I buried that guilt in my heart and didn't deal with it. Up until a few months ago, I didn't even understand that the hurt, the grief, the love was there. I'm sorry if it caused you pain, we should have shared it at the time."

He smiled with a lump in his throat, "Dianne, I never thought it was your fault. I just felt he was ill and God took him home. I think about him and pray for his soul every day. I have a Saint Christopher on my mirror, and every morning I kiss it and say a prayer for him." He paused a moment, "I've often wondered what it would have been like if he had lived."

With tears, I smiled and jokingly said, "We would have had four beautiful children!"

We both smiled.

I imagined because I had blocked the event out, I assumed everyone else had. I realized we all deal with grief differently and mine until recently was total denial. It was heartwarming to listen to Andrew tell me that he prays for Brandon every day. It was an emotional discussion; however, after thirty-six years, I believe it was healing for our son and any karma Andrew, and I had created between the two of us.

Thirty-six years, three plus six is nine, and nine is the number of completion. Once again this was God's Divine Timing.

Spirit Guided Me to Understand

Early March 2015 while working on the outline for the Archangel workshop, I was compiling information from various sources, when I heard a familiar name, "Doreen Virtue."

I wondered what that meant, why had I heard her name? I went to her website only to discover there was now a DVD for her ATP course that I wanted to take five years earlier.

I asked, "Archangel Michael, I've studied the work, should I take this workshop?"

Archangel Michael replied, "You learn differently from each teacher and is there not always something to learn."

It wasn't a yes or no answer, and I thought about this for several days and decided to order the DVD course.

When the DVD Set arrived, I was excited to get started, after I watched the introduction I discovered the DVD was recorded during a live workshop in 2012. I found a lot of the information was what I had already studied, but this was an excellent refresher.

What I realized, I related to the style of her teaching. The course gave me a deeper understanding of many things I had already studied. For several of the exercises, I had to enlist a partner. My friend Elizabeth down the street eagerly agreed. I also discovered to teach these methods you had to take this course and become certified in this program, you weren't allowed to use the same name, but you were allowed to use the teachings. I felt the Angels were helping me to stay within my integrity for future workshops to incorporate these teaching. As with any teacher once you complete their course you may use the information, but not the name of the course.

Toward the end of the course, she introduced her son Charles Virtue to the crowd. He told the students that he had discovered and had began working with a SIXTEENTH Archangel by the name of Nathaniel.

I found it interesting that another Archangel had entered to work with humankind, but that was about all I thought about it.

A few days after I finished the course I was meditating the color red entered my third eye, however, this was no surprise as I had been seeing red in my meditations for some time. When I asked Scott, he said that was the color he saw for Archangel Raziel.

So, as I had done many times, I said: "Hello Archangel Raziel, thank you for visiting me."

I heard an unfamiliar deep no nonsense voice answer, "No, it is not Raziel."

I wasn't afraid as I invoke Archangel Michael before I meditate, then I ask him to wrap me in his protection, as I step into a bubble of white light in my mind. I trusted that God, nor Michael would not abandon me.

In an assertive tone, I firmly asked, "If you aren't Raziel; who are you?"

The reply I received stunned me, "I am Archangel Nathaniel."

Immediately I saw the scene when he came to me on my drive home in 2014. I began asking him questions, "I am sorry I didn't know who you were when you first spoke to me. Why didn't you return?"

"I have been with you through your journey for some time. The time was not for you to know me, only to know of me. Creator is the origin of all time, now we will begin should you choose to work with me."

"WOW," was all I could say. I had just listened to Charles Virtue mention Archangel Nathaniel in a 2012 recording. Still, nothing clicked, I didn't make the connection. Yes I know I often tell Spirit, "I'm a little slow. Sometimes you have to hit me upside the head." However, I have come to understand these are spiritual seeds planted and when the time is right, they bloom. I was taken aback as I began to put it together. My new quest became "Who is Archangel Nathaniel, and why has he come to work with me?"

Through the days I discovered he had been making his appearance in my life for several years, immediately being attracted to the color red is one of the first signs he is there to work with you. Never in my life had I liked red. Blue had always been my color; red was just such a bold color. However, when we remodeled our home in 2009, I chose red as my primary color scheme which surprised my family. Another sign would be removing anything that is blocking your path, situations, and friends, which had also happened in my life through the last few years.

My expedition led me to this information: Archangel Nathaniel is known as The Patron Angel of Lightworker's and as The Angel of 2012. *I began my work with the Archangel's in 2012, interesting* was my thought.

Although he was here with us long before 2012 he appeared at that time to assist in the massive awakening of consciousness. Archangel Nathaniel is here to speed up our spiritual growth to raise the vibration of love on our planet; again I was in awe as I read this and the words rapid spiritual growth ran through my mind. He tells us we've taken enough workshops. We've studied enough, read enough books; it is time to get on with your mission.

Coincidence that we became acquainted before the Archangel workshop, remember I don't believe in coincidence. I mentioned Archangel Nathaniel to Ginger and Scott; neither had heard of him. I mentioned my encounter with Archangel Nathaniel to Sophie. Her comment was "When Nathaniel makes his presence known to you, be ready to saddle up and ride. Your growth and desires will become a reality swiftly if you choose to work with him."

I have come to understand that when you acknowledge and start working with Archangel Nathaniel, be ready for subtle life changes for your higher good. Archangel Nathaniel works through you. As with all the Archangel's, the transition is safe and protected.

I know he started working through me that day in 2014. You will step out of your comfort zone, trust me, but you will feel ready to do this.

As we approached the end of April, and the time to announce the next workshop which would be "Meet the Archangels." This workshop would be an introduction to the sixteen Archangel's that I worked with currently. I would give a brief history and their specialties with examples of my experiences with them. These would be examples of how easy it is to work with them. I looked at the calendar, and due to other commitments, May 16, 2015, was the first weekend I was available. I had to laugh, as I now understood the timing of Archangel Nathaniel, he is known as the sixteenth Archangel to come and work with us, and he had to be included in the workshop for lightworker's experiencing rapid spiritual growth to know him and get on with their missions!

The Archangel Workshop was unbelievable for all of us! Angel orbs and beautiful messages came to us that day. One of the students came up after class and asked me, "What Archangel is the funny one that jumps around like a leprechaun?" I knew instantly he was speaking of Archangel Raziel the Archangel of Spiritual Understanding. Raziel has told me many times, "Keep it simple. Humans have made it far too hard to understand their spiritual side." It was a fun, upbeat extremely high energy workshop, with lots of questions and connections with the Angels. I was elated to be in service to help others discover and explore their unique connection with the Archangels. I knew I was to teach others of the Angels and Archangels and Spirit would do the rest.

I had been called to teach, and it was my greatest joy!

The Spiritual Festival held many different evening workshops in the summer. I asked Tina if I could participate. After that workshop, she asked me if I would be interested in teaching one-hour classes monthly at the Spiritual Festival. I was thrilled!

In 2015 I continued with my Spiritual Practice from my home, monthly teachings through September at the Spiritual Festival, monthly Spiritual Gatherings, plus Ginger and I were writing our second book in The Balance Series. I blinked, and it was now December.

I had begun to get the feeling that the festivals were not my path for so many reasons and I had missed the last two monthly festivals.

However, this particular Sunday I received what I call a gentle nudge from Spirit to share a table. I wasn't on the schedule to hold a class when Tina came over to my table and asked, "Are you teaching today?"

I replied, "I didn't know you put me on the schedule, I didn't bring any information or my notes."

A little voice whispered, "You've got this!"

I sat there a minute, and she impatiently asked again, "I thought I called you. There's a room full of people up there waiting to hear about the Angel's. Are you going to teach?"

I hesitated, I knew that the information was inside me, but I always relied on note cards to keep me on track, but before I knew what was coming out of my mouth I said, "Oh what the heck, let's do this."

On the way up to the second floor, I chuckled as I heard Bubba say, "Fly by the seat of your britches kiddo, they won't let you fall."`

I opened the door and walked in about two dozen people turned and looked at me. I heard, "No sweat, we're with you!"

With confidence, I walked straight up the aisle to the front as I said, "Good afternoon, I'm Dianne Morgan, and I am a Mystic Intuitive Spiritual Christian. I'm here to talk to you about God, and his Divine Messengers. Sorry to keep you waiting."

That was to that date one of the best hour classes I had held. Two people followed me back to my table and others stopped by all had questions, all were seeking answers.

That night while brushing my teeth, and I was still in "ah, of my words." I looked in the mirror at myself, and then I smiled, I looked up and said, "Jesus, I proclaimed I am a Spiritual Christian."

I heard the elation of love in his voice as he gently replied, "Yes beloved, you certainly did!"

CHAPTER 18
How I Discovered, I Am a Mystic Intuitive Spiritual Christian

I understand that perhaps many of you reading this are not religious and I will say neither am I, but others would argue if I follow Jesus then I am. Please don't misunderstand me; I am not challenging, or judging anyone's beliefs, as I now understand there are many paths to finding God.

For me organized religion is one path to finding our Creator; it was just not my path; as I believe our Creator has no Religion. This is my truth and who I am. I had a knowing from an early age that our Creator existed and that we were all his/her children and that we could communicate with him/her. Perhaps that is because we pray to him/her and that would be useless if he/she couldn't hear us. That knowing we call Faith.

I was the age of nine, and I don't remember the sermon that day but yet I do remember the feeling I have held onto for a lifetime. The day I accepted Jesus into my heart as if it were only minutes ago. When the sermon was over the minister asked "If God is speaking to you today, take a few little steps. Are you ready to accept Jesus into your heart and be washed by his blood and forgiven of your sins?"

I felt the gentle whisper but I lingered in my seat when I heard "there is no fear." What was I afraid of? What was holding me in my seat? Was it fear, guilt or sin? I was nine how much sin could I have done? But the love that called to me was greater than my fear. I began to move slowly up the aisle to the front of the Church; I trembled as I walked and my legs felt as if they were bound in chains. I felt the heaviness in my legs as I waded through what felt like thick wet mud and I dragged these massive chains around my ankles behind me.

I heard this beautiful, gentle voice, "I have you." The same voice I heard when Kevin's boat tipped over.

It took everything I had inside of me to walk up the aisle. But I followed that voice of love to the front of the church to proclaim my love for Jesus and God.

I'm not sure everything that the minister said to me when I got there, I do remember he asked, "Do you accept Jesus into your heart, into your life?"

Emotionally I answered, "Yes."

The scene now in my mind, I turned and started back down the aisle, I no longer dragged the weight, or felt the heaviness I experienced earlier. It was as if the chains had been cut and vanished. I was not walking, I floated back to my seat, or the Holy Spirit carried me. Even though I was a child, I knew I would no longer be alone. I felt a presence alive in me. My baptism ceremony was the following Sunday; it was a feeling of being bathed in White Light.

Over the next several years I attended church every Sunday and Vacation Bible School in the summer, but through time I began to question the teachings of the church, I didn't translate God's word the way it was being taught. I didn't question Jesus but there were many rules that I just didn't believe were God's rules. One Sunday morning at the age of fourteen that same minister gave a sermon that shook me to the core. I heard him say as he pounded the pulpit, "If you believe you can do as you please and come here on Sunday morning and be absolved, you are hypocrites of Christ."

He went on to say that just because you attend church on Sunday doesn't make you a Christian. If you don't live the word of Jesus every day, you are a hypocrite!

I was a young teenager, discovering life, my parents drank, and I had already tasted alcohol and tobacco, so what I heard and understood was that I was a hypocrite! I wasn't sure what a hypocrite was, but I felt shame.

When I got home I asked, "Mom what's a hypocrite?"

She explained, "A hypocrite is someone that says they believe in something, but they don't follow what they say they believe. Why honey?"

"In church today the message was on being a hypocrite," I said as I grabbed an apple out of the fruit bowl.

"Oh, I see," she said, as she thought a minute on how to explain this to me. "Well, the bible teaches that being a hypocrite is a sin."

I must have looked confused, when she added, "Basically honey you pretend to be a good Christian only when you are in front of others. Also, when someone does the same thing, you look down on them and judge them. So you can't say you're a Christian and not follow the Christian beliefs. That would make you a hypocrite."

My immediate thought was *a sin! I don't want to be a hypocrite! But I don't follow all the Church's beliefs either. How can the church judge me as a hypocrite when God is the only judge?* This began an inner turmoil that would last most of my life.

After that episode, I attended less and less until I eventually stopped going to church altogether, did I stop believing? No, I knew the feeling of Jesus in my heart. I knew God and have always known within that there is something greater than we are. I have always had Faith in that Higher Power. I have always tried to follow the teachings of Jesus. I was in confusion as to the churches interpretation of what God meant. I thought *if we could just ask God or Jesus, we would have the truth, not someone else's version of it.*

At this point I began having my private conversations with God, not just prayers but conversations. I realized I didn't have to be in a building called the church to connect with him. I could talk to him anytime, anywhere.

I went through my teenage years in the Seventies, believing in the love and peace movement that started in the Sixties. I couldn't identify with the prejudices of the world, the labels put on people. I knew Jesus taught to have compassion for all, love everyone, don't judge others, help others if they needed help and be at peace with each other. I also believed that there is but one God, who went by many names. That made sense to me as there were many languages there would be many names for the Higher Power which I know as God.

There was a period in my life that I also stopped searching. I still believed, I prayed occasionally and I tried to follow what I felt was the authentic meaning of Jesus. I tried to do unto others the way I wanted others to do unto me. I believed I had good intentions and a good heart. I worked to be kind and compassionate most of the time. I didn't lie, steal or

232

cheat; those were three things that morally I knew were wrong.

I didn't judge others for their actions, but I did get angry with people. I sometimes forgave, but I didn't forget.

After my children were born and over a twenty plus year period, off, and on I visited different churches, different denominations. I was still searching for the place that I felt comfortable, a religion I could follow. I couldn't relate to ALL the teachings of any one religion. I didn't understand, if there is ONE GOD, how could there be so many thought processes and so many different beliefs and rules on how to find him and worship him.

In my fifties, through my awakening to my connection I began to study other paths, and again I found with spirituality just like religion there are many different teachings. One night I had been reading on Jesus the Ascended Master, and once again confusion clouded my mind, so many interpretations. I put the book down and rubbed my brow and thought, *Archangel Michael, there are so many thought systems, so many beliefs that it can become very confusing. I don't know what to believe, what is the truth.*

Then I walked outside and sat down under the stars. As I stared up at the night sky I began to talk out loud, "There are so many different thought processes and beliefs on how to find God. Some people find that closeness with him/her through organized religion, it works for them. But I question all the rules, not the words of Jesus or God, but the interpretation of their words. Is the journey discovering what those words mean to me? I understand Spirituality is a personal path of seeking to find and feel close to that Higher

Power. Isn't the one truth that there is a Higher Power and we are all connected to him/her? Don't we each have our unique path to finding the Source of All? One wouldn't be better than another, just different, and they all lead us to the same Creator."

I immediately thought of the Angel in my dream years back, as she was showing me two roads and said "This one or this one. One leads to the other and both will get you to your destination. One will be smooth and the other rocky. The choice is yours." I wondered, *is that what she was trying to tell me?*

I felt the warm energy of Archangel Michael around me. I heard his deep velvet voice, and I imagined what was a smile on his face as he spoke, "Oh dear one, do not buy into others belief's, for they are not your own. What resonates within your heart is your truth!"

Your truth is what resonates within you I thought then I asked out loud, "What is my truth? I do trust and believe in your true word God. Does that make me religious? I have never prayed to Jesus but pray in his name. I've thought that Jesus is the son of God all my life, and he came to teach us, to lead us to God's love and how to treat and love each other. I am confused, was Jesus actually God who came down to earth, or was he is an Ascended Master? Believing that, would that make me spiritual?" I heard no reply as I continued my conversation.

"Some call Jesus an Ascended Master, I understand an Ascended Master to be those that walked among man, that

234

achieved enlightenment while on earth, and taught their fellow man how to reach a higher consciousness. But there were others over the centuries that did this as well. So yes, Jesus in that sense is an Ascended Master. When Jesus said, 'I am the son of God,' was it metaphorically, because we are all your children?

When he said 'I am the way,' does that mean Jesus gave us the answers to find you? He didn't say 'I am the *only* way.' Oh, so many questions!" I paused and sipped my iced tea and then continued my conversation with Spirit desperately wanting someone to give me the answers.

"Father in the cavern of my heart, there is a knowing and love of Jesus. I have always believed and tried to live his teachings. I've just never understood the fear based teachings of God. Does that mean Jesus is my teacher or my Lord? But if I don't believe he's the only way does that mean I am not a Christian?"

As I spoke, I realized I had created an internal mess for myself.

When I discovered the metaphysical world, it was all so new to me and led to many questions. I met new friends that were Spiritual, but they also introduced me to their beliefs. I went through many thought processes, and the more I talked to others, I began to wonder if I had been wrong all these years, I questioned everything I had ever believed about Jesus. I no longer knew what my truth was. This confusion led me to look deeper and continue my Spiritual Journey to find answers to my questions.

Through the years I explored and discovered my connection with the Spiritual Realm. I found I could communicate with Archangel Michael, and then I began to connect with other Archangels. Why not? I communicated with God. I had daily conversations with them as I went through my Spiritual Growth. I knew I was communicating with God's messengers. I believed it was all Divine Guidance. However, my Christian friends didn't think that I was talking to Angels. I had one friend tell me I had to be talking to demons because we can't talk to Angels and the devil disguises himself as God's messengers.

Many times, I had the same question for Archangel Michael.

His answer was simple, "Do not buy into others beliefs for they are not your own. What resonates in your heart is your truth! Search within dear one, and you will find your truth."

My trouble was I no longer knew what resonated in my heart. Just as the teachings of the church, there was information in Spirituality that I believed and others I didn't feel were the truth. I felt I was so new to the Spiritual path that surely all these people knew more than I did. There had to be one truth, didn't there? How could I be Spiritual, and Christian? How could I talk to Spirit and be Christian? But Jesus heard God and the Angels speak to him. Jesus said, "Very truly I tell you, whoever believes in me will do the works I have been doing, and they will do even greater things than these." This verse translates to me that I can communicate with the Heavenly Realm.

I have discovered that what I was searching for was inside of me all along. I thought I would walk into a church and find it there. My Spiritual Journey led me to understand I would

236

never discover that undying love, that overwhelming joy in a brick and mortar building. Nor would I find it through someone else's truth. ᚗ

It was in that meditation in 2014 that Jesus came to me, I saw the glory of his beauty and I recognized his face. The face I saw as a child.

When I saw him, and fell to my knees, I felt incredible guilt that it had taken me so many years to understand him. Guilt for not knowing he was always there leading me. When he wiped my tears and wrapped me in his embrace, smiled down at me and whispered in my ear, "I have always been here waiting."

I experienced such tenderness, and forgiveness as my heart burst open with love so pure and deep-seated. I was overcome by his presence as he opened the eyes of my heart. I felt complete. I was whole and overflowing with utter joy. I had been asking and searching for my truth. I never understood it had been inside of me all along. I accepted the love of Jesus as a child when he came as my friend, my brother, my teacher. I had found my way home, following my inner path through his teachings. I found the answer I was seeking lived in me.

I thought about his visit many times, and I began to share this experience with my Spiritual friends and speak my truth. To some my beliefs didn't matter, for others they slowly drifted away. For me, I had had so many beautiful experiences with Jesus through my life I could no longer be confused as to who he was to me because in my soul I knew my truth. It had been so many years ago, and he had been there patiently waiting for me. All the time he loved me, talked to me and remained there for me to find my way back to him.

I had let myself become confused as to who Jesus was for me. I now realized that he could also be called an Ascended Master, he did live as a human man, he did help others and did great deeds through his earthly journey. I now understand and realize Jesus was a Spiritual Teacher, he was a Mystic. He walked the inner path to God and he understood the Christ within and found enlightenment. Jesus didn't come here to create a religion, he came to show us how to find God's Light within ourselves and reach enlightenment. I now understand for me, Jesus is my Lord, my brother, my teacher, my friend. I have imprinted his words in my heart and my soul, as something inside of me changed that day.

I have learned to love all things, to share the joy of Jesus in my heart by shining my inner light of God. This light lives in all of us, and I had to walk my journey to find it. We all have a unique journey to find the Christ Consciousness that lives within each of us. Had I lived in another place, or another time, perhaps it would have been Siddhartha Gautama Buddha, or Paramahansa Yogananda, or Quan Yin, or Allah, or White Buffalo Woman, or Ganesh, or Vishnu, who came to teach me. But Jesus came to me. My younger brother once told me he was Spiritual, not Religious, he belonged to a Christian Church, I didn't understand what he meant, but nor did I ask.

I felt I wasn't Christian because I didn't follow the Church's beliefs and rules. Then I confused myself by listening to the belief's of others because in reality I now understand I to have been Spiritual all along, and through His Grace, he saved me from myself.

238

Once I became aware I worked with the guidance of Creator and his beautiful Divine Messengers. I took my journey to a deeper soul level, asking questions and continually going deeper and deeper within myself; the healing was liberating. This was not an easy task. However, for me, there was no other task. I believe my soul agreed upon this long before my mind accepted it.

Through connecting with Spirit, I now understand who I am, my heart sings to be in service to others, as I continue my teachings, writings, and energy healing work. For me the translation is simple; the Spiritual Journey is you discovering your unique connection by "Going Where They Are," and Discovering Who You Are. Connecting within your heart and finding your truth, not following someone else's interpretation of truth.

It took me fifty years to come to that conclusion. Even though I do not follow any outer religion, I found a magic in the inner silence, and I can hear the whisper of Spirit. I know I have talked with Jesus and heard his voice many times in my life. If I said, he was the only path then wouldn't I be in judgment of others?

Jesus came to teach his followers; I am one of them. I believe in what I can't physically see or there is no intellectual reason, therefore I am labeled a Mystic. I communicate with Spirit, I am Intuitive. If we can communicate with God, and he/she being the Highest Power, then why wouldn't we be able to have conversations with Jesus, Archangels, Angels, Guides and Deceased Loved Ones?

As I walked my path I found Jesus waiting there. I don't belong to any organized religion. Organized Religion is

239

beautiful if that is your chosen path, just as Spirituality is wondrous if that is your path to find your truth.

I followed my intuition and what resonated in my heart. I choose Spirituality, my personal path to finding God, Creator, Great Spirit, and Source of All. I followed my heart which was led by the love and teachings of Jesus in hopes to find enlightenment to return to God Spark. Mystic Intuitive Spiritual Christian may not be the correct term. However, it is mine. After all, it's just a label; a title to give you an identity for others to understand who you are. But does anyone ever truly know your heart?

My prayer is that my story will help others realize that Spirit connects with each of us every day, twenty-four-seven, in our waking hours and our dreams. In writing my story, I began putting all the events in the perspective that it was Spirit at work in my life. I have found that everything on our journey is synchronicity. Everything is Divine Timing. I also pray that you will recall and reflect on events in your life that you know some other Power intervened. Or perhaps these writings help you understand you aren't crazy, that you are connected and that you now have a knowing and it is real. Spirit is guiding you, helping you through thought, feeling, sound, or seeing. Protecting you, loving you and wanting you to find happiness.

I believe when God said 'let there be light,' he was speaking of his light that shines within each of us. When Jesus said, 'you are the beckon;' he too was saying 'Shine your light of God for all to see, leading others to find him within themselves.'" For me those words are why we are united Lightworker's, but then again that is my interpretation.

Go Where They Are, is my story, finding my truth and shining my light for all to see.

"I am fire that ignites a spark within others which creates a flame so that they may shine and pass the torch…. I am a Lightworker.

Namaste

ANGEL NAVIGATION

You Have Always Been Connected to the Spiritual Realm

As a child, most of us are told; you didn't see that or that didn't happen you must have imagined it. That what we see or hear which is not right in front of us for all to see and hear isn't true or real. We're discouraged from communicating with spirit ('s). Think about it. After being told over and over again, one would stop believing it was real. When we are children our parent's, and other adults know everything, we believe what they tell us. From my own childhood experiences, a child begins to doubt themselves and doesn't explore their connection. I call this attunement to denial. This thought leads me back to my idea of children and imaginary friends. Because no one was physically present, could it be a spiritual being or a guardian angel? I don't think they're imaginary at all.

 As children, we are innocent and open before most parents and society unintentionally shut down our third eye. It's hard to believe something when others doubt it.

Once belief systems block the veil to Spirit through our parents our teachers and some organized religions, the connection begins to fade from our thought process because we are taught it's wrong and not real. Eventually, we don't hear, see, feel or know that angels and guides are there because we have blocked them out. It's like turning the sound down on the radio. It's still there just not as loud.

I choose Spirituality, which is a personal path of my own connection with Divine Spirit. I talk to God and Jesus and the Angels, and through my clairs, I hear them.

I do not believe that our loving Creator would have given gifts to a chosen few. We all have these gifts; we are all born with the ability to connect with the Spiritual Realm. How do they connect with us? Religious or Spiritual, we All hear God, in our prayers, meditation, and through our family and friends. Many have worked to build a stronger connection and know they understand God, Jesus, Angels, Archangels, deceased loved ones. It is simple, acknowledge your unique communication and practice it.

We connect with Mediumistics better known as our Clairs, the French word meaning 'Clear.'

The white wolf that I saw as a child, even if it was in my mind's eye, the scene with the dog chasing the bicycle; the dreams I had of my grandfather in the automobile accident and my dad's funeral and Mark and the car chase. These are examples of **clairvoyance.** Clairvoyance may be the way Spirit speaks to you through pictures in your minds' eye. Clear 'seeing' in your head or outside your head, the visions occur during waking state, in meditation as well as in your dream world.

During that scene of the white wolf, I also heard my name called as it rushed by me. Then another time when I heard "I've got you. You're okay," when the boat tipped over. I've also heard the Angelic Choir from out of nowhere, when I asked Mark, "Who is singing?" He turned the television down and listened then looked at me; I still heard the beautiful sound of Angels singing. However, sometimes Spirit speaks to you through others. An example of this would be: after my Spiritual birthday party and Bubba's favorite song came on the radio and confirmed to me, yes they were there. When you are asking for answers, and a song comes on the radio, it may be a message. Messages could come through something you're watching on the television or you over hear someone talking that gives you the exact answer you needed. These are all examples of **clairaudience.** Pay attention once you ask a question in your mind or through your voice. Clear "hearing" is interpreted as hearing outside of your head. However, Archangel Michael has told me that sometimes hearing the Spiritual Realm is inside your head and sounds like your own voice.

My first pregnancy and knowing I was pregnant when the doctor said I wasn't. My third pregnancy and being told I was having a boy and knowing it was a girl. Knowing my mom would survive pneumonia but that Bubba wouldn't survive the motorcycle accident. In 2003 when asked how I handled mom's dementia and I said I just "Go Where They Are." It wasn't until 2014 I understood this was the title of this book. When I asked for another name for "brain fart" and received "Spirit Burst," which became the name of the newsletter, then later became the term I use to describe a message from Spirit. These are all example of **claircognizance,** in my mind I just knew. I have had friends and family come to me for advice most of my life, and I have somehow always known what to tell them. Also, having the Spiritual knowledge I've never studied pop into my head. Clear "knowing," not knowing how you know, you just know. Spirit drops the information in your head.

We all have that gut feeling or a hunch that something specific is going to happen and it does. Or maybe you have a sense that you need to call someone, or do something and later discover the call or action was literally what was needed. Perhaps you've had an eerie feeling that someone is around you, but there is no one physically there. Or suddenly you feel heat, or coldness around you when the temperature hasn't changed, this is known as **Clairsentience** or clear "feeling." You sense the answers, messages, and guidance from heaven or I like to call it, feeling Spirit.

These aren't the only ways that Spirit communicates with us.

Clairalience is known as clear "smelling." I experience this with my mom and her juicy fruit gum, or Wind-song perfume. With my dad, it's his tobacco or the smell of barbeque. This communication comes through a lot with deceased loved ones. Floral fragrances I have identified with the Angels. Don't disregard a scent, there maybe someone visiting you.

Clairgustance is known as clear "tasting." I don't experience this one but do know people who do. They have explained as suddenly having the taste of something that the deceased person liked or disliked. It is the ability to flavor the food without putting something in your mouth.

So many things we don't think about are messages from Spirit. I have also understood that we are born with one "Clair" that is stronger than the others. However, through my personal experience, I know that by exercising and working with each of them you can strengthen them.

5 Tips Develop Your Clairs for your Spiritual Growth

Meditate as often as you can for at least 10 min daily

Work with tools, such as cards, crystals, pendulums, explore all the tools and find what you feel works for you.

Practice, Practice, Practice

Study-read, read, read whatever appeals to you.

There will be times that the messages make no sense, write it down, keep a Journal; eventually, you'll know what the message was telling you.

Why Positive Affirmations

Your thoughts, feelings, words, and actions create your reality. What we desire comes from the heart. Your heart is your Spiritual Connection.

For over the last ten years I have studied and applied many metaphysical thoughts and practices into my life. I only know what worked for me which fueled my desire to teach others how truly connected we all are. The journey is to explore and discover your unique connection.

We receive what we desire by drawing it to us by the Universal Law of Attraction. Your positive thoughts, words, and actions are what make it possible to achieve those desires. When you think or say, "I can/can't do that! I do/don't hear Spirit! I AM or AM not connected!" Two things come into play the Universal Law of Attraction and your Free Will!

246

1) The Universe won't bring anything to you that you don't see for yourself! Jesus has said, "Think of the Universe as a mirror, when you look in the mirror and frown what do you see looking back at you? Hence when you look in the mirror and smile, you receive a smile looking back at you. You attract what you put out." It's pretty simple.

2) You have Free Will, and God will not disobey his law of Free Will. Your words tell God you do or don't desire to do these things.

An affirmation is a declaration of what is. Therefore, if you yearn for something in your life, you must declare that you already have it. Putting I AM in front of your desire is stating that it is so. It requires time and patience as nothing is instantaneously, and everything has to be for the highest good for all involved. You may think nothing is happening, but trust the Angelic Realm is working behind the scenes to help you, and the outcome may surpass your greatest desire. Ask, Believe, Trust, and Receive.

Also understand that if nothing happens, then this may not be the right time, person, place or thing for the highest good of everyone involved.

Affirmations are important as you create your reality with your thoughts, actions, and spoken words. To start your day with positive thoughts, I want to share with you Affirmations I use daily for my Spiritual Growth.

I consecrate this day to Christ Love; I consecrate this day to Christ Perfection.

I can easily hear and understand the inner voice of Spirit.

I AM Fearless free of Fear and Doubt

I AM Protected

I AM Clairvoyant; I connect with spirit through sight

I AM Clairaudient; I connect with spirit through sound

I AM Claircognizant; I connect with spirit through knowing

I AM Clairsentient; I connect with spirit through feeling

I See, Hear, Know and Feel Clear Divine Guidance

I AM Blessed

I AM Growing Spiritually

I AM Abundant

I AM Supported

I AM Divine and Perfect Spiritual, Physical Body, and Mental Health

I AM Walking my Divine Life Path, with God, Jesus, and the Angels

I AM Grounded in the Light

I AM Happy

I AM an Intuitive Communicator

I AM Beautiful

I AM Strong and Confident

✓ I AM an Energy Healer

I Am Grateful

Anything you desire can become your Positive Affirmation.

Are you ready to Meet the Archangels?

Archangels are family, they are friends, and they want to be involved in our lives, from the minuscule to the enormous. I invoke them daily. I call this Hiring my Angel Teams for everyday events as well as my desires.

If you don't do so already, then I encourage you to get to know them. I am thrilled by the presence of the Archangels in my life; I give them reverence. I say please, and thank you, but I do talk to them the same way I talk to anyone. They speak to each of us in a language we will understand.

I AM HONORED TO INTRODUCE YOU TO THE ARCHANGELS the way that I see them and the way that I teach them by their halo colors.

What a Fun way to learn about Archangels! I have also included some of my personal experience that I have had while working with them.

Should the color not resonate with the energy you feel for this particular Archangel, I ask you not to disregard your feelings. I also understood that the Archangel's change specialties every one hundred years, therefore, it would make sense to me that we may see them in different colors based on when we began to study and your connection with them. Being humans, we tend to hold onto our belief systems of what we have learned.

249

If there is not a color that you have connected with, please know that doesn't mean that there is not an Archangel with that halo color, or another Light Being wanting to connect with you. There are thousands, wanting to communicate with us.

I had been seeing a lime-green for sometime but it was only recently I was drawn to study the dragons. Only to discover the lime green I see is a mixture of pale green and gold and is the Water Dragon, which according to Diana Cooper is of the fourth dimension and they maintain the constant movement of the Christ Light in the waters of our planet. When I mentioned it to a few spiritual friends, they have also been seeing that color. For Archangel Metatron, I always saw a mixture of pinks and greens but was told his color is orange. With the Archangel Gabriel, I see orange; others say copper represents him. I wonder if that is because he is portrayed as carrying a golden trumpet. Deep within I believe there is no right or wrong color, just your unique interpretations of their energies and the color as it appears to you.

These mystical messengers from God are pure love and want us to be happy, and they desire to help us find joy in life. I find them to be extraordinary, helpful, loving friends and companions. Talk to them; invite them to help you, after all helping you is one of their greatest pleasures, because helping you is being in service to God, which in turn is in service to you.

I introduce them by colors, and perhaps in some small way that will help you connect. From experience, I can tell you if you are suddenly attracted to a color you have never really admired, look at what is happening in your life and see this as the sign that a particular Archangel is around you and wanting to help you.

Remember they are omnipresent, meaning they can be with as many people that call on them all at the same time. They also do not belong to any particular religion, as God isn't a religion.

Angels, just as everything, are energy. Energy is ever flowing and can never be bothered. Energy is tireless. Energy is what creates halo colors. Archangel Metatron asked that I explain in my teachings that Angels don't have wings. When I asked him to explain why this is, the short version of his answer was this; "Centuries and centuries ago when the Angels appeared to give God's message to man, it was thought they came from the sky. In that time, birds were the only things that flew in our skies. So, it was assumed God's messengers had wings and illustrated as such throughout our history. Each vibration of energy generates a different halo color the higher the vibration, the more vibrate the color.

I have learned in working with Spirit that the Archangels, Spirit Guides and our Angels do not make decisions for us. They are happy to guide us to make the best decisions that we can and drop signs to lead us. If the request is meaningful to you, it is meaningful to them. However, you must ASK. No Light Being will disobey God's Law of our Free Will.

I wish each of you spiritual growth as you get to know the Archangels.

The Archangel Color Guide

Blues

Light or sky blue represents Archangel 'Raguel' whose name is said to mean 'Friend of God.' He keeps situations fair and balanced between you and others including, relationships, business, friendship, and family; especially the relationship you have with yourself. Working with Archangel Raguel helps you find the harmony in life, for the highest good of all.

Examples of working with Archangel Raguel; with the Type 'A' personalities in my family, any time we have a gathering at my home I call upon Archangel Raguel for relationship harmony and I trust there will be no arguments. When I have to tell others truths that aren't what they want to hear rather it be family, friends or business I call upon Archangel Raguel for harmony between all concerned.

Dark Blue, Royal Blue, Cobalt Blue, Royal Purple these colors represent Archangel 'Michael,' whose name is said to mean, 'He who is like God.' Michael was the first Archangel created by God and is the head of all the Archangels and Angels.

I see Michael's orb as a beautiful cobalt blue. However, the colors listed above are identified by others, as it's his energy you cannot mistake. Commitment and dedication courage, direction, vitality, motivation, all the aspects of our life purpose are Archangel Michael's specialties. Michael is known for his protection of our human bodies and our spiritual bodies. Clearing your space of lower and negative energies is also one of Michael's specialties. If you've seen blue sparkles or flashes of light those are a sign of Michael near you.

I have many stories in working with the Archangel Michael. One of my favorite stories of Michael is the mechanical angel. We are accustomed to relying on computers, electrical and mechanical tools in our life. If it malfunctions, it can cause unnecessary stress. Yes, that's right Michael will help you with mechanical issues, either repairing them or leading you to someone that can repair them. My example was our washing machine, the knob to start the washer was stripped and needed replacing; my husband looked at it and then told me I needed to call a repair man. Later that evening I wanted to wash a load of clothes. I stood in front of the washer and tried figuring out the knob, and it occurred to me there has to be a way to engage it.

I said, "Archangel Michael, please help me figure out how to start the washer?"

It did not surprise me when I heard, "Push down and hold it with one hand and turn it with the other."

I did as he explained and the washer started. I laughed, and said, "Thank you Michael." to which I heard, "My Pleasure."

You should have seen my husband's face when I told him Archangel Michael and I started the washer. No, he didn't come down from heaven and repair my washing machine. It may have been something any mechanical savvy person would have figured out. However, everything in me knew it was Archangel Guidance that helped me that night.

Indigo Blue is the color for Archangel 'Zadkiel' whose name is said to mean; 'Righteousness of God.'

Archangel 'Zadkiel's' helps us focus on the beautiful memories we have made and forget the hurt and pain which in turn is an emotional healing. This healing is for the forgiveness of self and others. However, he too has other specialties, not only can he help with memory and forgiveness, he is a 'spiritual professor' Archangel Zadkiel will help you remember information you need when you ask him for help, in teaching and writing.

Archangel Zadkiel is also one of the Archangels to call upon for heightened clairaudience by clearing your ear chakra's so that you may hear the Divine Messengers.

I don't know that I could have taken this cleansing alone, going within and forgiving myself and others without the help of Archangel Zadkiel who has been with me through the writing of this manuscript. I cried many tears during these writings as I realized it was a deep healing that was occurring. Thank You, Dear Zadkiel, for I am emotionally healthy from working with you.

Iridescent Blue/ Pale White represent's Archangel 'Haniel' whose name is said to mean 'The Glory of God or Grace of God.'

Archangel Haniel has been proclaimed the 'Goddess of the Moon' in many cultures going as far back as the Babylonian era. Archangel Haniel will help you with heightening your Spiritual gifts as she helps you open your intuition and third eye and trust your inner feelings and guidance, living up to your highest potential. She also helps facilitate physical healing and emotional heart break; and feminine issues.

I have worked with Haniel for some time in developing my spiritual gifts, simply by calling on her. I first discovered her as the angel of the moon and began working with her during the full moon. I light candles and call upon Archangel Haniel asking her to heighten my spiritual gifts, facilitate physical healing, and Evoke Divine Grace within me. I have experienced a gentle breeze wisp through me as I stand under the moon and talk to her. I feel in my every being this is Haniel's sweet embrace.

Copper, I see this as a brownish Orange represents Archangel 'Gabriel,' although in some parts of the world I have heard them use white as the color for Gabriel. Archangel Gabriel's name means 'The messenger of God or strength of God.'

I call upon Archangel Gabriel the excellent communicator, as he helps us speak our truth lovingly, in giving us just the right words to deliver. Helping writers, speakers and teachers are one of his specialties. I also call Gabriel the motivational angel as he helps with procrastination issues and gets you started on your dreams. Gabriel is also the protector of all children, and can help with conceiving and parenting, should you need guidance in that area.

When I have a fussy grandbaby, I call upon Archangel Gabriel to help me soothe and calm the child.

In all of my writing projects I talk with Archangel Gabriel explaining what I am trying to relay and ask him to give me the words, the words begin to flow; I created the term "Angeltation," to describe how it works for me. I also call upon Archangel Gabriel to assist in teaching.

255

Deep Green colors resonate with Archangel 'Raphael' who's names mean 'God Heals,' or 'He who heals like God.'

Archangel Raphael again has several specialties but is most well known as the supreme healer in the Angelic realm. His healing encompasses all healing issues; physical, mental, emotional and spiritual. Archangel Raphael also works with anyone in the healing profession, traditional and alternative healing. He is also known as the travel angel; rather it is as simple as finding a parking spot to safe travel for an upcoming trip.

I ask Raphael for safe travels every time I get in my vehicle. I also call upon him when I pull into a parking lot simply by saying, "Archangel Raphael, parking spot please and thank you." One night in doing energy healing work on my sweet fifteen-year-old Jack Russell, I called upon Archangel Raphael and his healing band of angels, as I looked down at my hands, his emerald green energy was flowing around her.

Orange is known for the Archangel 'Metatron.' However, I see Archangel Metatron as a mixture of *violet and green* swirling together. Archangel Metatron's name is said to mean 'Next to the Throne of God' it is said he sits next to Gods head.

One of two Archangel's whose name does not end in el. The ending 'el' means of God. Archangel Metatron works with all who ask for help with their spiritual transitions. He will give you strength and keep you on the right path of your journey. He keeps you organized and helps you accomplish priorities by keeping you focused.

Metatron works closely with sensitive children. With this in mind, I explain and recommend Archangel Metatron to teachers, and parents, especially parents of Crystal and Rainbow Children as they are very perceptive of energies.

Being that Archangel Metatron is said to be the prophet Enoch and walked the earth doing great deeds as he achieved his enlightenment, he is accessible to all of us because of his dedication to teaching the practical application of esoteric wisdom. Which he has explained to me in short as: "the hidden wisdom your soul came in knowing and the spiritual journey is finding that wisdom within yourself." Hence, he helps us with spiritual understanding.

Working with Metatron in my teaching, the message I received was to "teach the children." I believe we are all God's children and with so many awakening, guidance is needed to help them to share their contributions to better themselves and all kind, meaning humans, animals, plants, and Mother Earth. Without guidance, their gifts could be used to harm others, or they would shut themselves down because they did not understand the gifts. Our youth look to us the adults for guidance. One of my decisions to teach was when I heard, "if not you, then who?" I believe that goes for all Lightworker's and why I am devoted to helping others with their Spiritual Growth.

PINKS

Pale Pink is Archangel Ariel, whose name is said to mean 'Lioness of God.'

Archangel Ariel is known as the Angel of Nature and pictured with two large lions by her side; with her love for nature she works with environmentalist and preserving and protecting our planet, nature, and animals. However, Ariel has other specialties amongst them is helping with Physical Manifestation for your Life Purpose physical needs. She can help you find compassion within for others while standing your ground, using healthy boundaries and not aggression.

To continue moving forward on my path I call upon Archangel Ariel during New Moon, asking her to help me manifest my physical material needs for my life mission. New Moon is said to be the most opportune time for beginning a new cycle of manifestation. I also have asked her for help with animals and plants, with results that I knew were divinely guided. No, these were not miracles; however, I believe and trust that the information was given to me to aid them.

Pale pink is the color for Archangel Chamuel. However, some identity with a light sea foam green, I often wonder if this is because Chamuel works with Archangel Raphael in the healing of the heart. Chamuel's name is said to mean, "He who sees God."

Chamuel has a never-ending vision, and he sees the connection between all people and things. For short I call him the GPS Angel. One of his specialties is to help us find everything we are searching for in life. Relationships, careers, the right place to live, and lost items. Call upon Archangel Chamuel to help you find patience, understanding, forgiveness, and love which is all inside of you. Chamuel is also the Archangel of Peace, righting wrongs and helping find justice for all. Call upon Archangel Chamuel for all that you are seeking.

I have many examples of Chamuel's help, but I think my favorite is the story of the lost keys. Years back Anne and

Chad (her first child) were visiting, arriving on Monday and they were scheduled to leave on Thursday. Chad was about the age three at the time. On Wed. Anne mentioned leaving and Chad insisted he wasn't going home.

He said, "No, I stay with Nene." Anne and I chuckled over his cuteness, but his words warmed my heart.

On Thursday morning Anne packed and started to load her car when we discovered her keys were missing. She searched all day for those keys with no luck. We had decided that I would get up early Saturday morning and meet my son-in-law half way (an hour and a half) and pickup the extra set of keys.

On Friday evening, I was downstairs alone, when I asked, "Archangel Chamuel, please help me find those keys. I do not want to get up at 6:00 AM and make that drive."

I heard a soft voice say, "Look in the recliner."

I yelled upstairs to Anne, "Did you look in the recliner?"

"Yes, Mom,"

"She's already looked there," I said.

Then I heard again, "Look in the recliner."

I walked to the living area and began to stick my hand down into the sides of the recliner. Nothing!

I muttered, "There's nothing there."

I then heard, "Check toward the back."

I pushed my hand down the back of the recliner and then heard something hit the floor.

I bent down and looked. The keys were lying on the floor under the chair.

Of course, I walked up stairs swinging the keys, "Where'd you find them?"

"Archangel Chamuel guided me to them in the back of the recliner." We both laughed. Anne was awestruck and me, well I was in gratitude of showing others just how simple it is to work with the Archangels.

Dark Pink or Deep Rose Pink is Archangel 'Jophiel' whose name is said to mean, 'Beauty of God.'

Archangel Jophiel, the angel of beauty, has a distinctly feminine energy. His mission is to bring beauty to all aspects of life. When you call upon him, he will assist you with beautifying your thoughts, your feelings, decorating your home, keeping the energy flowing positive and even to help you pick the perfect outfit or hairstyle. If you've had the thought of cleaning a closet or drawer, it is usually a sign that Archangel Jophiel has entered near and desired to work with you to de-clutter your life. Most do not realize when we hold onto things; we are creating stagnated energy; nothing flows when it is still or trapped. We can't move forward without letting go.

Working with Archangel Jophiel can help you quickly change your mindset from a negative to a positive thought. You can say, "Jophiel beautiful thoughts please and thank you." You will notice that the negative process of reflection slips away.

He is wonderful to call on to help heal misunderstandings with other people.

Call upon him for anything you want to beautify; relationships, environments, or life itself. I feel that when you notice the beauty of the world, these are all signs that Archangel Jophiel is near and reminding you to see the beauty around you.

When I don't know what to wear, I ask him to pick out my outfit; and I will hear a color, such as blue, then my thoughts or eyes go to a particular outfit.

Dark Purple or eggplant purple is the color of Archangel 'Jeremiel' whose name means 'Mercy of God.'

Jeremiel surrounds those that are trying to make changes in their lives, just waiting to be asked to help. He will assist in conducting life reviews of your path good and bad so that you may move to the next transition in your life. He helps you develop an understanding of spiritual visions and clairvoyance. Jeremiel is a teacher and a mentor who can guide you to see yourself and others with love. Jeremiel also helps us stay focused on our Divine Life Mission. "Dear Archangel Jeremiel, thank you for leading and helping me, so my path is clearly understood for my life purpose," invokes his presence.

My first encounter with Archangel Jeremiel was early on in my awakening when he appeared in meditation, I saw the egg plant purple halo, and I asked "who are you," I heard "Jeremiel." I wondered why Jeremiel came to me, which had me studying all aspects of him, and understanding within all of us lives a shadow side. We must review and embrace it as part of who we are to move forward on our path. Jeremiel helps us identify and make changes in our life to lead us to our Divine Life Mission of Service to others. I worked with Jeremiel understanding myself, others and my purpose this lifetime. After teaching workshops, myself, I have discovered with many experiencing their awakening; after Archangel Michael, one of the first Archangels the students met was the Archangel Jeremiel. Jeremiel also works with us and life reviews once we transcend to the other side.

Rainbow represents Archangel 'Raziel' whose name is said to mean 'Secrets of God.'

His halo glows with the colors of a rainbow, like a beautiful prism of color. For me this explains the crystal associated with him being clear quartz, when the light hits the quartz it becomes a spectrum of color.

I find Raziel to have a comical side, as he says we take things too seriously. When I began teaching on the Archangels, Raziel spoke to me and suggested, "Keep it simple." As he explained, Our Creator, Spirituality, the Angel's, it's all straightforward. We are all here to guide you to find the love you hold inside. Creator desires your journey to be of his/her Love for you. Through that Love, and compassion you share the love for each other, you help each other, by being in service to those in need and you will find the joy in life. Working with Archangel Raziel, he will help you work on your dreams until you manifest them into reality. He holds the secrets of life and can help you with spiritual understanding and the esoteric wisdom of the universe.

Raziel is an excellent teacher. Archangel Raziel awakens the spiritual knowledge (esoteric wisdom) we each brought in with us. Raziel will explain it to you using words that make sense to you. A language that you understand making it so very simple, and FUN, because it is! WE make it hard. When I was developing workshops, I was often reminded, "Keep it simple."

Red is the color for Archangel 'Nathaniel' whose name is said to mean 'Gifts of God or God has given.'

Archangel Nathaniel is also known as the 2012 Archangel and the Lightworker's Angel. He assertively pushes you to work on and go after your life purpose. Nathaniel eliminates people and substances in your life that do not serve your life purpose. While working with Archangel Nathaniel, I have discovered he is very to the point and shows up when it's time for you to get on with and do what you came here to do.

He helps us move forward on our life path and shows us the things that are keeping us stuck. Unlike the others, Archangel Nathaniel works directly through us, lovingly nudging us to take action. He asks us to keep believing in our dreams and goals so that he can help us to manifest them, always for our highest good.

Turquoise is the Archangel 'Sandalphon' whose name is said to mean 'Brother.'

Sandalphon helps all in the fine arts, music, artist, authors, songwriters, and actors. Also, he can give you the gender of unborn babies if you ask. Sandalphon delivers our prayers and brings us the answers from Creator, or as I like to explain it; "Archangel Sandalphon carries our prayers from our lips to God's ear, and returns God's esoteric wisdom to us in a language we understand."

There was an experience when I called upon Sandalphon and ask that he deliver my prayer, I looked up to the sky and saw what looked to be a turquoise thumb up sign floating up to heaven. I have also asked Sandalphon for the gender of my grandchildren, which I believe has surprised my family when it is correct.

Pale Yellow is Archangel 'Azrael' whose name is said to mean 'Whom God Helps.'

Azrael helps us through all transitions in life through the Grace of God. Reminding us that there will always be beginnings and endings as this is the natural flow. Azrael works closely with counselors and grief counselors. One of his duties is to escort souls to the others side and stay with family during the bereavement period.

There are always, new relationship, new homes, careers, divorce, children coming and children leaving home and death. Our lives are full or change, and we experience a transition period during that change. He helps us acknowledge, and deal with the fact that endings and beginnings are natural.

I call on Azrael when someone transcends, to be with the ones they have left behind. When I did mediumship readings for those, who have recently lost loved ones Azrael comes through with loving words. I call upon Azrael to guide me with all stressful endings and beginning in my life. Don't confuse the name with Azazael who is considered a demon or fallen angel. Though I have not met Azazael, I have heard their energies couldn't be more different. God's messengers are pure and trustworthy beings of his/her light which can't be mirrored by other spirits.

Yellow is for Archangel 'Uriel' whose name is said to mean, 'He who is the light of God,' and 'The Fire or Flame of God.'

His specialties are many, Bright ideas, Creative insight, Recall of knowledge and Focus; because of these specialties he is known as the 'Intellectual Archangel.' He is wonderful to call on when you need solutions, in business, for a test, in writings. He whispers the correct response and answers into your ear or mind. After you ask Uriel notice your thoughts, you'll suddenly receive words, thoughts, or pictures. What I like to call as "Downloads." He can also help with releasing negative thought patterns. Known for his ability to enlighten our minds, Uriel answers all who call upon him.

I have called on upon Archangel Uriel to lighten my spiritual path to help me find my way; to awaken the spiritual knowledge or hidden wisdom in my soul. Whenever I ask a question of him, and the answer comes, my first thought is "Thank You, Uriel, for the Bright IDEA."

Below are a few other colors that I see and feel are important to share. Some of you may be seeing them as well!

Gold is the color I see for Jesus.

When your aura is open, such as in meditation, I invoke Archangel Michael, and I also ask Jesus to surround me in his golden light of total protection.

Some see Archangel Michael in a golden light as well, what resonates with you is your answer, everything is interpretation. Jesus taught of Father/Mother God's Love and of finding Peace through that Love. If you are finding difficulty in Clear communication with God, Divine Guidance, and direction, faith issues, forgiveness, healings of all kinds, manifestation, and miracles, all you need do is ask for his help.

Fuchsia, this is representation of 'Mother Mary.'

Divine Feminine and also known as the 'Queen of the Angels;' some know her as an Ascended Master. Mother Mary will help with adoption of children and all other issues related to children. Fertility, and all related feminine issues. Mother Mary also performs healings of all kinds and shines mercy to you. She will help you open your heart to compassion.

Magenta is the Archangel 'Mariel.'

After seeing the color in meditation, I once again was on a hunt. My studies led me to Archangel Mariel, who works with us in opening our eighth chakra. The eighth chakra is the soul star chakra also called the seat of our soul. The eighth chakra is a few inches above our crown, which radiates our Divine Feminine wisdom. Mariel also assists in energy healing work.

White – represents our beautiful Guardian Angels

Here's another example of Spirit helping us when we ASK.

When I get in my car, I asked the Archangel Michael to protect my vehicle and the Archangel Raphael for safe travels.

On this particular day, I had been to the grocery store I pulled into the drive, Mark came out to help me unload, as I was getting out of my SUV I stepped down, my feet slipped out from under me. It was like slow motion. First I landed on

266

the running board. Next, I bounced on my derrière to the ground!

Mark came running around the vehicle expecting to find me in blood or knocked out. He asked, "Honey, are you okay?"

As I sat there a minute and took account of my body, I laughed and answered, "Yes, the Angel's broke my fall." I felt them catch me. Honest, it was like someone caught me and slowly sat me on the ground.

So, the moral is "Say it! Think it! Write it! Visualize it! And Affirm it!" any way you do it works, just ASK for their help.

Daily Spiritual Maintenance

Spiritual Health is an essential part of the Lightworker Spiritual Practice. The subject is taught under many different titles. I choose to call and teach it as Daily Spiritual Maintenance. Once I received the Spirit Burst from Archangel Michael on Spiritual Health, I began my practice morning and night, and when needed throughout my day. Before that, I did it occasionally when I felt the energies of others surrounding me, or if I remembered. When I was working on outlines for workshops, Archangel Michael always reminded me to teach the importance of Spiritual Health.

There is light and dark in everything that is why it is important to protect your energy. It was when Archangel Michael said and asked, "As Lightworker's you are very sensitive to all the energies around you and the world. You're like sponges, you absorb. You must realize Light Energy attracts Lower Energy, and Chaos is a lower energy. Why then aren't you practicing daily maintenance?"

I realized I must share it with everyone I met. As Archangel Michael explained, energies don't only come from others; dark forces are negative energies that feed off the light, so you don't have to be in a crowd to attract dark forces. I picture it as the energies are flying around, and then they see the light shining in someone, and they surround that person to increase their energies. I don't know about you, but I need my light energy and asking Michael to clear, shield and protect me is important.

I also might add I learned a lesson on shielding when you ask Archangel Michael to shield you, remember your words. "Archangel Michael please shield me, allowing only messages from the Divine," will keep the communication with the Spiritual Light beings open. Of course, you may word it any way you choose and if there is a deceased loved one that you wish to communicate with including them in your request. Once you have made it clear, in the future it's easy, all you say is, "Shield Up."

What is the importance of cutting emotional cords? We all form cords of attachment with others. You are sensitive to your environment, and pick up energies even doing kind deeds for someone you form an emotional attachment; which allows you to pick up their energies. Repeating patterns in your life could be caused by a cord of attachment to a person, place, or thing. Anything you keep returning to, even though you know it's not good for you.

In my interactions with others, I ask Archangel Michael to cut cords sometimes several times a day.

Invoking Archangel Michaels Protection and Shielding can be as simple as saying "Archangel Michael, please surround and protect me. Shield me from all lower energies. Thank You."

I also learned something else about shielding. You may call upon Ascended Master El Morya and ask that he shield you from your negative thoughts and ignite your internal shield of protection from all lower energies. This shield will stay up until you ask him to remove it. That bewilders me, why anyone would want it removed.

I love ceremony, and therefore I invoke the Deep Blue/Purple Cloak of Protection As learned from the teachings of Diana Cooper– "Archangel Michael, please cover me with your cloak of protection." Imagine or see Archangel Michael wrapping you in his cloak from head to toe.

Invoke the Golden Ray of Christ also as learned from the teachings of Diana Cooper; you do not have to be of the Christian Religion to invoke the golden ray. "I Invoke the Golden Ray of Christ for your total protection." Say this three times and as you call upon the golden ray, imagine it as a golden cocoon of light surrounding you.

Imagine or see a big white bubble, as you walk into the bubble say "I am totally safe in the pure white light of God."

Now I am ready; I have Michael's cloak; the Golden Light of Christ and I am walking in the light of God.

Grounding is a term used in Spirituality meaning centering yourself in your body. Not being grounded would be the feeling that you can't concentrate, feeling spacey, scattered and unfocused, flighty with your thoughts and actions. There are many methods for grounding, and the more often you

269

practice grounding, the easier it will become to ground yourself. Here are a few tools; there are many for grounding, find one that works for you.

Meditations – my favorite is the roots coming out of the bottom of my feet going deep and connecting with Mother Earth

Dominate hand up against a tree

Walking barefoot on grass or sand

Wearing Crystals like Hematite, Smokey Quartz, Black Tourmaline can help with grounding

A few Examples of Daily Spiritual Maintenance

Ask Archangel Michael to cut any cords of attachment that connect you with others.

Ask Archangel Michael to remove anything from you that is not of God.

Ask Archangel Jophiel to bring you beautiful thoughts

Ask Archangel Raphael to heal your heart and help you forgive yourself and others.

Ask Archangel Raguel for relationship harmony with all you know and meet.

Ask Archangel Gabriel to guide your words that they are loving given and received.

Ask Jesus to help you walk in love and compassion

Ask Creator to let you see as he/she sees

Ask Archangel Michael and his Mercy Band of Angels to take all negative energies that surround Mother Earth and transmute them and return them to us as Positive Loving Healing Energy.

Whatever Light Beings you work with 'Ask' them to be your maintenance team, and when you find yourself short on time call upon your team, "Maintenance team you know what I have asked and what I need, please and thank you."

A Quick Charge

When you are out and about and start feeling the energies, silently say "Archangel Michael, please clear me inside and out." Once your body feels calm, say "Archangel Michael, please Shield Me." Or "Thank You, Archangel Michael, for shielding me." They both have the same effect.

On a final note: Are these practices out of fear, not at all, this is Spiritual Maintenance so that I may continue my journey of being in service. It's like taking an umbrella with you in case of rain.

Archangel Michael said, "These practices aren't something you do once in this lifetime. Nor do you do them every once in a while. You eat daily, and some pray daily, why then haven't you developed a practice for your Spiritual health?"

Archangel Michael says "WE all have much work to do here and you must take care of self to serve others. Love yourself the way Creator loves you. Love yourself enough to practice a daily spiritual maintenance."

Acknowledgements

Thank you first and foremost to our loving God, Jesus, the Archangel's, my Guardian Angels, Ascended Master and Spirit Guides, without you in my life this story would not have been written. Thank you also to my family and friends for your encouragement to complete this book, and the love you have given me along the way.

To Elise Krentzel who taught me many lessons.

To Teresa Hawley Howard, and her team for all they do, I am so blessed to have been led to you.

Last but not least, thank you the readers for reading my story and I pray you enjoyed the journey as much as I enjoyed recalling it and sharing it with you.... You have your own story to write, or perhaps to remember..... I pray that in some way I have helped you the reader realize you can "Go Where They Are," which in reality is all around you.

Writing and releasing "Go Where They Are" was a new path of my journey with Spirit.

The path of sharing with the world who I am and what I have learned. The Angel Navigation section is but some of the teachings Spirit and I do in the Connecting with Spirit and Let's Talk Angel workshops. *May the information be of benefit to each of you on your unique path!*

THIS IS ONLY THE BEGINNING

Not

THE END

Find additional information exercises and meditations in our next book "Angel Navigation"

Coming in Divine Time

Until then I'm sending Blessings of Love and Golden Healing Light to ALL on

Angel Wings.....

Dianne

Author Bio

Dianne lives in Canyon Lake, Texas with her husband; she is a mother of four and grandmother of seven grandsons. Dianne is a Mystic Intuitive Spiritual Christian; an Ordained Universal Life Minister, a member of International Association of Angel Practitioners as she holds certifications as an Angel Intuitive, Angel Therapy Practitioner, Reiki Practitioner and Crystal Energy Practitioner. Dianne is a Co-Creator and with Spiritual guidance 'Angel Navigation LLC' was born. She and Spirit developed 'Intuitive Crystal Angelic Energy Healing.' She is a Spiritual Teacher and Speaker, where she helps others to discover, explore and strengthen their unique connection to the spiritual realm.

I love my life and the opportunity to be in service to others. I am dedicated in helping others grow spiritually and the healing arts. We ALL have the gift of being connected it is simply recognizing your connection and working with it. Like a muscle the more you use it the stronger it gets. *Working with Spirit is uplifting and exciting!* Following this Divine Guidance, we can bring Unity, Love, Compassion, Peace and Joy to Earth for All kind.

Contact Dianne at www.DianneMorgan.com

Facebook at
https://www.facebook.com/diannemorganangelnavigation

Twitter at https://twitter.com/AngelNavigation

Other works by: Dianne Morgan
Co - Author of the Metaphysical Thriller
Writing team 'Morgan Shores'

The Balance: Awakenings
The Balance: The Return

Dianne Morgan is also a co-author in WOM Publishings

His Grace is Sufficient

And Coming in 2018!

The Power of our Voice

The Power of Prayer

Angels Among Us

Warrior Women with Angel Wings Born to Love

Ps M, 2J, Rev 4 (applys inbetween eyes)
Clear seeing (prepare in oil for 3-7 days)
687 882 17?
Ps 29, 19, 58 (7 days in oil)

— (((

— tiiba eni esa

— Tolu adimut

Day 3 — breaking out to go and worship god
an assistante by (him) to drive me but I later
took over from him because he was tired and
wanted to go back home. I eventual picked the
car somewhere and trecked all the way to the
worship center. I saw a diceased friend. I
brought out my garment which I had a long time
it was stained with the beverage I carried
along with it. Pastor mrs Adesanya helped to
wipe the stain. surprisingly it became not only
clean but New and different. The service
already started I was still delaying to eat
etc.

Manufactured by Amazon.ca
Bolton, ON

Ps 28, 27, 4 eni okun

client.equfash.ca